# 21 Adventures & More

Allie Breitenberg

21 Adventures and More
Copyright © 2022 Allie Breitenberg
All rights reserved.
ISBN: 9798836807559

First published in the USA by Amazon.

No part of this publication may be reproduced or distributed in any form
or by any means, or stored in a database or retrieval system, without the prior written permission of the author.

Cover Illustration by Matthew Hall
Interior Layout by Janna Barber
Printed in the United States

Twenty-One Adventures & More

# IN MEMORY OF LILA KATHRYN MCALISTER
## 3/31/2010 - 1/9/2015

LK is my best friend forever. She smashed a whole lifetime of love, light, and laughter into four and a half years. LK was known for bear hugs and small pats on the back, which were often topped off with a "wet baby kiss." She had a unique enthusiasm about life that she shared with everyone. After spending time with Lila Kate, I always felt like I'd been given a healthy dose of happiness and love.

Twenty-One Adventures & More

Twenty-One Adventures & More

# TABLE OF CONTENTS

Part 1: Meeting, Knowing, and Loving Lila Kate

| | |
|---|---|
| Adventure #1 - Simply A Small Coincidence | 10 |
| Adventure #2 - Meeting Lila Kate | 13 |
| Adventure #3 - Unique Connection | 16 |
| Adventure #4 - More Playdates | 20 |
| Adventure #5 - One of Those Days | 23 |
| Adventure #6 - The Greatest is Love | 26 |
| Adventure #7 - Write, Write, and Write | 28 |
| Adventure #8 - Early On in My Grief Journey | 33 |
| Adventure #9 - The Smallest Tools | 36 |
| Adventure #10 - Grief Unfolding | 41 |
| Adventure #11 - Inflatable Man/ "Aftershocks" | 45 |
| Adventure #12 - A Special Tool of Investing | 48 |
| Adventure #13 - Hurting and Hurting Some More | 52 |
| Adventure #14 - An Unexpected Blessing | 58 |

Part 2: Reflecting on Some of My Favorite Journal Entries from 2015 - 2020

| | |
|---|---|
| Adventure #15 - The Halfway Point…I thought! | 61 |
| Adventure #16 - The Hardest Words to Write | 68 |
| Adventure #17 - Too Much | 70 |
| Adventure #18 - Dealing with Anger | 72 |
| Adventure #19 - His Goodness Doesn't Change! | 74 |
| Adventure #20 - Storm | 76 |
| Adventure #21 - God Gives and God Takes | 80 |
| Adventure #22 - I can | 83 |
| Adventure #23 - LK's 7th birthday | 87 |
| Adventure #24 - Allowing Myself to Be Weak | 90 |
| Adventure #25 - Grief and Depression | 92 |
| Adventure #26 - Gloomy Days | 96 |

| | |
|---|---|
| Adventure #27 - Children's Books | 99 |
| Adventure #28 - Church Family | 102 |
| Adventure #29 - Share | 107 |
| Adventure #30 - Life | 109 |

Part 3: My Life Now, and How I Still Struggle Sometimes

| | |
|---|---|
| Adventure #31 - February 18, 2021 | 114 |
| Adventure #32 - February 19,2021 | 118 |
| Adventure #33 - February 26,2021 | 121 |
| Adventure #34 - March 14, 2021 | 123 |
| Adventure #35 - March 20, 2021 | 127 |
| Adventure #36 - April 9, 2021 | 129 |
| Adventure #37 - April 14, 2021 | 133 |
| Adventure #38 - April 20, 2021 | 136 |
| Adventure #39 - April 30, 2021 | 139 |
| Adventure #40 - May 13,2021 | 142 |
| Adventure #41 - May 15, 2021 | 145 |
| Adventure #42 - May 20, 2021 | 147 |
| Adventure #43 - May 23, 2021 | 150 |
| Adventure #44 - June 4, 2021 | 153 |
| Adventure #45 - June 6, 2021 | 156 |
| Notes | 166 |
| Acknowledgements | 169 |
| Author Bio | 172 |

# FOREWORD

"Wow! Audrey and I were just talking about her ... and you, earlier. Audrey was talking about some of the silly things she used to do. We had a good laugh. My back has been hurting all day (I've been miserable and probably not the most pleasant person to be around) and I needed that smile it put on my face. She still has a way of affecting & reaching us to this day. (Only God does things like this. He's still working through her).

I'm not sure what genre of music you usually listen to, but "Pieces" by Gary Allen (that'd be country) makes me think of LK. It talks about how everyone that comes into your life shapes and molds you ... no matter what, when, where, why, or how they come into your life. LK softened my heart and soul. I needed that especially at the time that I fell in love with her.

She is the main reason that you and I met. Yes, I knew who you were. Yes, you were good friends with my nephew, yes you were an icon on Lakeside's campus, yes I thought highly of you, but my first thoughts when I think of you is when I reflect back on your friendship with LK. Y'all's relationship is the main reason I became so interested in you. We shared that love for her. I couldn't understand why I felt so strongly about her but I knew that you did, too.

Now I'm a fan of yours, too! You are such an inspiration to me. You are so wise, caring, full of love, and just downright amazing (especially for your age). You help renew my faith in not only our youth but also humanity in general. I think the world of you. Thank you for being who you are and being my friend."

~ David Puckett, a good friend (June 2016)

# INTRODUCTION

The word adventure is defined as being "engaged in hazardous and exciting activity, especially the exploration of unknown territory." Yes, hazardous and exciting, and sometimes all in the same breath and it's exactly the word I'm using to describe my first writing process and self-publishing! In general, this book is a book of "mini adventures" spanning the years of 2010 to 2021, and my prayer is that God will use each "mini adventure"—no matter how "hazardous" or "exciting" the terrain might be—to point my reader to His "greater adventure" of redeeming mankind. I pray my reader simply sees more of Him…more of His goodness, faithfulness, and love, because all three aspects and more are always present; no matter how unpredictable, unwanted, or unpleasant the terrain. How do I know? I know because He is always present.

If I was going to define the word adventure, I'd lean towards each adventure being more exciting and less hazardous. That's just my personality. But unfortunately, no one has asked me to submit a noteworthy definition so I'll try to flow with such. Just keep swimming, right? Or better yet, just keep climbing, with your head held high, and a humble attitude. The task of climbing is a better comparison for this rough terrain that my reader is about to encounter with me.

Indeed, I've learned that God has used my writing as an outlet for my grief journey and a platform for me to express my faith. But the idea of publishing a book sounded far beyond what I was capable of, so when others would encourage me to do so I agreed it was a cool idea, but I didn't know how to go about accomplishing such a task. For a few years the idea simply came and went without me really pursuing the whole book idea. I had quite the collection of writings under my bed and every time I would sit down to ponder the idea of writing a book I would feel too overwhelmed with my emotions and slide the binder back under my bed. The idea of publishing a book seemed to come to me as quickly as it left. But at the same time in the back of my thoughts, I knew God was already using my writing to be a source of encouragement to me and others, due to me sharing bits on social media. I've always told myself if one person is encouraged through me sharing my journey then the heartache I've felt is worth it. At the same time, I knew God could open more doors to more people if He wanted, and I wasn't totally opposed to that thought either.

So in the early months of 2020, I was continually asking God to expand my story so I could expand His greater story; His story of pain, His story of beauty, and His story of redemption. I was curious about how I could reach out to others and what I could do to make a difference in another's life in a new way. It had to be in a new way because that is when we were experiencing stay home recommendations due to COVID-19. The whole global pandemic of 2020 could be a book in itself and will probably be in digital textbooks one day; it was history in the making for sure! I wrote continually throughout this time, not about the crisis our world was facing, but God did allow me to capture some noteworthy words about the COVID-19 season. I placed into my notebook the following:

*Yes, this is indeed a dark moment in history but I'm recalling the actual darkness that fell upon the earth when Jesus died. I'm reflecting on what God did through that darkness and how it points me as God's child to my brightest future that awaits me, and to the light that He calls me to continue to walk in as I await that glorious future. That darkness was needed to accomplish what only HE could accomplish. And what He accomplishes is only good for His children, just as a Father because He's our Heavenly Father.*

Those words were being played out in front of the world, and it's safe to say those words hit me on a personal level, too. Especially when it comes to saying "see ya later" to my all-time best friend. Lila Kate is pretty much my "why" for writing my first book as I so desperately wish that my reader would've had the grand opportunity of hugging the sweet and sassy little love bug and receiving a pat on the back, but maybe this will serve in part as a "virtual meet and greet," for she's now exploring the vastness of Heaven on a daily basis. She has been doing so since January 9, 2015 and sometimes it feels like it has been forever, while other times it feels like just yesterday.

Yes, even to this day my grief still experiences those "shadows of death" (Psalms 23:4) moments which are obviously dark, but too (sometimes together) I still experience the Light. The light is because of Jesus. Jesus is the Light and Jesus will always be the light. The darkness will not and cannot overpower the light (John 1:5). Lila Kate was indeed a reflection of God's light and God's love.

Below is a beautiful description of Lila Kate, written by Maggie Trieshmann:

*The whole room was drawn to Lila Kate. God gave her a beauty that no one else could quite capture. She knew how to make anyone and everyone feel special and loved and she took pride in that. She loved her mommy and daddy and looked up to her big brother and big sister so much. You could see it in her eyes as she watched them play. Watching her laugh would make you laugh and watching her cry would break your heart. She was created so beautifully in God's image and He was shown through her daily. You knew that just looking at her. She had a divine purpose, and she fulfilled it. When that was over she went to make people giggle and smile and feel important up in Heaven!*

The story of Esther wiggles into my thoughts when I reflect upon the timing of this book. Of course Esther was up against greater odds, but I don't think God tends to fall into these comparison traps the way I so easily do. Yes, thanking God for His grace all along the way. Let's see with Esther, at large the story serves as a picture of the feeling of God's absence but the truth of God's continual presence all throughout. Which is exactly what Jesus experienced for man's sake upon the cross, for there Jesus felt alone, but truthfully and thankfully God was still there.

During Esther's years, it was also a dark time period for the Jews who were experiencing captivity and probably thought all God's promises were completely forgotten. But as noted through many of the prophets, God's hand is clearly shown through the physical hand of a person. In this case it's Esther. An interesting fact about the book of Esther, is not once is God made reference to, yet over and over one continues to see His redemption work unfolding, specifically in the life of Esther. God uses her to stand up for the sake of her people...for the sake of God's people. She could've easily sat with her emotions (dating all the way back to childhood) and not rise up to the task that God was equipping her to do, but she heard the encouraging words of her uncle Mordecai, which are echoed here: "For if you keep silent at this time, relief and deliverance will rise for the Jews from another place…. And who knows whether you have not come to the kingdom for such a time as this?" (Esther 4:14)

God's timing is completely everything! A time for everything and for everything a time, there's a summary of the first part of Ecclesiastes in two sentences! And this is not the last time I will mention God's timing, because it really is everything! Anyway, Esther could have kept silent, because after all her assignment involved risking her own life. Or on the flip side (which was the right side too), Esther could've taken the chance while leaving the outcome in God's hands. Esther did the flip side and today you can, too. To me, writing my first book was my flip side. God stirred this story to share which maybe was to be shared for a time such as this. I pray it'll serve my reader as a reminder that darkness will not and cannot overpower the light, as well as paint a picture of the feeling of God's absence, while still displaying the truth of God's continual presence.

All my years in grade school, writing was always my favorite. I was eager to write and a bubble of excitement actually built up in me when I was asked to do a research paper! Of course research papers weren't my favorite, but I remember looking forward to exploring and learning something new. For I see now that's part of life, exploring and learning along the way. My favorite task was writing narratives. One might say they are the easiest to write, I thought the same thing, until writing this book. The writing process was difficult (especially my first go around) and it was a big trusting process with God as well as an aid in my healing process. These words here aren't easy to share, but God never promised easy for His children—instead He promised for His presence to be with us continually. So through this book God has allowed me to share my grief journey this far of seeing Lila Kate run to Heaven and for me to share how He has proven Himself again and again as my anchor of hope with His ongoing faithfulness.

Even when I wasn't in the classroom, I had an early love for writing. One memory from my childhood involves Ethan (my brother) and I drawing/writing on his bedroom wall. Of course it was his room, but it was probably my grand idea. I'm sure we were acting out the mysterious hand like in the book of Daniel; except it wasn't mysterious! Mom was on the phone and apparently we thought it had been a long enough phone call so we were getting restless. We decided to practice our writing skills. Great idea, but not when it comes to the bedroom wall. Mom came looking for us probably because the silence was too loud. I'm glad I don't remember dad's reaction, but scrubbing those walls wasn't nearly as fun as writing love notes to each other. I know it's a negative example, but my reader can see my love for writing from that childhood memory!

On a positive note, as I grew up, I graduated from writing on the walls to continually trying to fill up a notebook. My notebooks date back to 2010 with Bible journaling, prayers, and the day's highlights. Even to this day I find great delight in laughing and crying through my past notebooks. It's in my notebooks that I see how many times God has been faithful. Spoiler alert: There's not a time where He hasn't been faithful, nor will there be!

All throughout the years, my parents took my brother and I to church so I had the privilege of hearing the gospel from a young age. It was one particular summer Vacation Bible School where I felt God's tug for my personal need of repentance and I realized my home was in Heaven! But a pivotal point in my journey with Christ would be around 7th/8th grade. It was then when God "accidentally" crossed my path at the gym with this personal trainer who I didn't even know at the time, nor had I ever experienced a conversation with him. But as it played out, God used this particular person to stir my heart towards His Word more and that's when I began to intentionally invest in my personal relationship with the One who has always known and loved me completely. And He does you, too! This is simply the first of many random accounts with people whom God purposefully placed along my path to show me again that there is no such thing as "random" with God! Still to this day my favorite "random" with God involved Lila Kate! Lila Kate loved and loved some more. Lila Kate will always be my best friend and through this experience with grief I wish I could say that pain only makes one stronger or it does get better with time. And while I suppose it does in some minor degrees; I continually remember that this is a fallen sinful world that's probably growing more sinful by the day yet Jesus came knowing that fact and still loving us; His prized creation (James 1:18)! When I have that as my focus; I can continue to go on.

Jesus came from Heaven and lived the life that I couldn't—He lived and lives a perfect life. He came knowing beforehand that the agony of the cross would be necessary in order to repair our relationship with Him because that relationship was destroyed when sin entered the world. Jesus suffered and died on the cross, but to keep His promises true, He was raised to life on the third day! And now because He lives, we can live too, even after dying. He invites all to turn from their sinful ways, ask forgiveness, and trust that He is truly enough, with life forever in the perfection of His presence. And that's the hope of the gospel, which keeps me going, as well as the gift of other priceless friendships He has given me—the best one still being my friendship with Lila Kate.

# Part 1:
# Meeting, Knowing, and Loving Lila Kate

# ADVENTURE #1 – SIMPLY A SMALL COINCIDENCE

It was one of those small coincidences that seem so random at the moment, but all these years later I realize that small coincidence was the exact way God wanted to show me more of Him, even though it involves pain. There's no such thing as coincidences. As I go back to the beginning of this short season, my heart still floods with a craze of painful emotions, but also with the evidence of God's perfect timing, His enduring faithfulness, and His ongoing comfort.

Cade Hill, our former Associate Pastor of the church I attend, and a close family friend, has been preaching through the book of Ruth recently. Cade pointed out that Ruth's story is full of random little "coincidences." Ruth was a Moabitess, an outsider to the Jewish nation. Her husband died and she returned to Bethlehem with her mother-in-law Naomi. In chapter two, Naomi encourages Ruth to go gather the leftover grain in a certain field. And by "coincidence" this field is owned by a relative of Naomi's…one who could redeem Ruth and provide for her and Naomi. While this seems to be a coincidence, we know this can't be the case. Because everything is under God's control; there aren't any coincidences in life. As I see in Ruth's story, the owner of the field, Boaz, ultimately falls in love with Ruth and marries her.

These two become great grandparents to King David and therefore in the direct ancestry of Jesus Christ himself. Ruth's story ultimately points to Christ and how He came to redeem mankind. Ruth is another glowing light in the Old Testament, in the midst of the darkness of her circumstances.

With that backdrop, let's take a walk down memory lane, back to the time when I was in middle school. I'm in 6th grade, walking the hallways with a trombone that is bigger than myself…yikes. That's my favorite part of the day, then adding hundreds of more legs, and arms, in the hallway, it's definitely my favorite part! But hey, it's the last bell of the day and that's pretty much all students' favorite part of the school day. I'm not in a hurry to get out front to wait for mom, because it usually takes her a handful of minutes to leave her school building where she helps with younger grades. I didn't mind waiting, especially on days that Mrs. Misty McAlister, a Seventh grade teacher, was on car rider duty. She's the one that noticed my uncomfortable hallway experience, so she allowed me to wait close to her and she would always load my trombone for me. In a way, this was kind of going against school rules, because I wasn't waiting in my assigned grade area, but I had permission to bend the rules.

The following school year, I had my heart set on getting Mrs. McAlister for a seventh grade teacher but Open House night came with the crushing disappointment of getting placed in a different class. Of course, I would be compatible with a different teacher, but I had my heart set on Mrs. McAlister. Nonetheless, my homeroom teacher was the next best, and I quickly adjusted to the new school year. But for some reason, God kept Mrs. McAlister on my radar and I was thrilled He did. Maybe it was in the halls that I learned my favorite teacher was pregnant with her third child and that she would be out of school for a long time. I asked mom about the situation, as she was now in the school office most days so she could easily find out. We found out the scoop that Mrs.

McAlister was on bed rest, which obviously entailed complications that followed. This was March of 2010.

Surprisingly, I survived my seventh grade year without my choice teacher and now was extremely nervous about moving to a new building in the Fall, for I had made another favorite teacher. It seems as though every year, I wrapped at least one teacher around my finger and they did the same with me. I always found ways to escape the craziness of the cafeteria, hallways, and yes, sometimes even fire drills. Yes, I was the troublemaker, and I will totally admit it! My high school principal would, too.

Anyway, before 8th grade kicked off, I was somehow given the opportunity of what I now consider an opportunity of a lifetime in meeting Lila Kate McAlister. I had no idea that she would instantly become my best friend and that I would fall in love with the entire family! My reader has to forgive me for I don't recall all the exact details in meeting LK but God obviously did, and still does today, which is more than enough. I reflect today knowing His hand was orchestrating the entire process (as He is always doing so).

# ADVENTURE #2 – MEETING LILA KATE

"Come meet her, she'll love you!" Mrs. McAlister said. Of course, I immediately fell in love with every ounce of the baby girl. Yes, the typical baby vibes were clearly present, but something else, too. I'm lacking the words in my description but there was something more than simply a general "meet and greet" that day, and for that I will always be thankful. At the time, summer was ending and Misty (LK's mom) was about to gear up for another school year. Misty learned that I had an eye for organizing and we made a plan to go work in her classroom the following week, which became a tradition of ours during most school years. Following our work day in the classroom, she asked if I wanted to go play with LK? Of course, I did! She was home with "Nana" (Margie) along with her big brother and big sister. As I came to find out "Nana " was the one usually keeping LK during the weekdays so LK wouldn't have to go to daycare, which made things easier for the whole family!

This baby had a diagnosis of Down's Syndrome, which at the time I didn't know what that fully meant, even to this day I don't know all the ins and outs of Downs, but I did get to see it play out for four and a half years. And it's the "thing" that my heart aches for the most. When I met Lila Kate, I didn't see her differences, I saw love and pure happiness. Yes, she was on oxygen, but that was the only visible thing, and even that she didn't seem to mind too much. But as I spent more time with the family, Lila Kate did indeed experience fits like a typical baby, especially when she yanked out the oxygen tubes. The oxygen was needed around the clock, because the pressure on Lila Kate's heart was slightly increased.

The diagnosis of Downs usually comes with a handful of "other" diagnoses, particularly issues with the heart or lungs. For example, Lila Kate was born with a hole in the center of her heart (Atrioventricular Septal Defect, or ASD for short), which resulted in a need for open heart surgery at the age of three months old. With Down's Syndrome, individuals are given a full or partial copy of Chromosome 21, and in Lila Kate's case it was simply a partial copy, which meant she wasn't as severe. By the time she was two-years-old, doctors saw that Lila was improving with each visit, so they proceeded to encourage her parents to "go show that little girl off to the watching world." But let's backtrack, God gave me a little sneak peek, because when I met Lila Kate she was about one- year-old. I realize this now and I'm so thankful for this, especially on the harder days! It was like the "backstage" pass to see a famous actor or your favorite musician! I say this, because Lila Kate's immune system was very fragile and her parents had to be extra cautious of who was around their daughter. At the time, I met her, I wasn't aware of her health conditions nor the possibility of us instantly connecting, or that I would soon be calling her my absolute best friend! But God did, and that's always enough!

# ADVENTURE #3 – A UNIQUE CONNECTION

There was a unique connection between Lila and I that God instantly allowed to explode, but I wasn't fully aware of it at the moment. With my eighth grade fall semester kicking off, I was actually amazed at the easy transition to the new building. Of course, I learned how to "sweet-talk" all my teachers and stayed on their good side most of the time. There were a handful of instances when I found myself in trouble due to laughter; isn't laughter good for the soul? I'll admit it was usually at the wrong moments and bad influences from classmates who were some of my favorites, as we tended to always see trouble together.

Anyway, most Friday afternoons I could be found going home with the McAlister clan. My tagline quickly became

"Friday Night Date!" Upon arriving at the McAlister's house, we usually found LK sitting in her Daddy's lap or taking an afternoon snooze. Regardless, Skip (LK's dad) continually declared that hand washing was mandatory before coming in contact with the beautiful love bug. This was before 2020. If she was awake, LK's sister Annalise, usually swooped her away from Daddy and with a cheerful voice would say, "Allie is here." I would make my way to the couch where LK would join me, and welcome me with her now famous "LK hugs." They were the kind of hugs one simply wants more of and the kind of hugs, which I couldn't get enough of. She was part monkey in some cases, because she would actually climb on me to hug me. I'll say she gave "bear and monkey hugs." Maybe the "monkey hugs" were when she became more active and realized she could push up with her legs. I'm not sure, but I took it as her unique way of communicating to me that she missed me and loved me!

Like most children, LK went straight for my glasses and the phrase "hands down" became useful in teaching her not to grab. I took great pleasure in joking with Skip, as I would ask LK about his and her tasks for the day, otherwise known as mom's *honey-do list*. As I asked, Skip probably rolled his eyes while we giggled. This became a popular question on Friday afternoons, and Skip caught on quickly, so he would be completely comical with his answers. The big kids (LK's siblings) usually had friends with them after school, but periodically we would all play together with LK. She loved when the big kids played with her, especially the boys. LK's brother Thomas, was an amazing big brother, (as was Annalise as a big sister) and they would both always watch out for their little sister.

As the clock quickly ticked by LK and I found the big blanket on the living room floor where we spent hours playing together. The books were our favorite. I took delight in making Lila laugh and seeing her smile as I turned the pages. We would jump into the books and I would imitate the characters while using different pitches of voices, which Lila loved! Whenever she would laugh, I would laugh! Another activity that resulted in laughs was building towers with soft blocks. I would build a tower and Lila would knock it down as we both laughed. A seemingly small thing to laugh at, but I'll never regret a laugh with Lila! I would have to build the tower speedily because by the time I had maybe five to six blocks, she was ready to bring the windstorm.

As I rack my mind for memories at her young age, I realize they consisted mostly of playdates on the big blanket with toys. One of her favorite toys was the bear who sang the classic song, *head, shoulders, knees, and toes*. Luckily, we captured this on video, and even though watching it floods my heart with a rush of heavy emotions, I'm so thankful we have that live snapshot to look back on. That was one of our *things*, Lila and I always took pictures, usually multiple snapshots were required at each play date. It wasn't until after she went to Heaven that I realized how important these little snapshots were. It was as if God was preparing me all along. He was preparing me for the unthinkable, the unimaginable, and the unwanted.

# ADVENTURE #4 – MORE PLAYDATES

The first time I was trusted to give Lila her bottle, everyone knew, I was part of the family. Skip was especially particular in her feedings, and anything else that involved Lila Kate, which was almost everything! To her various medications, to the minor adjustments of her car seat and stroller. Each Friday afternoon, Misty and I would set a reminder for Lila's medicine, so she would stay on schedule.

As Lila became more active, we wondered when she would start walking, and joked around that her dad would have to build a *Segway* system along the ceiling so Lila's oxygen tube could slide along without getting tangled. But God had different and better plans. When Lila turned three years old, the oxygen tank quit following her around the house. It was the best birthday present ever! Just a few days before she had her cardiologist appointment, which came with the best report yet! The pressure on Lila's heart was decreasing so this meant the oxygen tank was only needed at night now. Everyone bubbled with excitement, though I'm sure it was a bit nerve wracking making the transition, but she did well. This memory is one of my favorites so my reader will come across it again!

Lila quickly showed everyone she was free of her oxygen tubes! Skip and Misty began taking her more places and she was quick to add a spark of love in every heart she encountered. LK's hugs became known at church. Along with her waves at the bank, grocery store, and yes, even the car wash! Lila always went to the car wash with her dad! Lila wanted others to know that they were loved! Once at summer church camp, a particular camp volunteer met LK and spent time with her. Afterwards he commented, "That girl taught me more about love in three days, than I had ever known." That's the legacy Lila Kate left upon this big beautiful world that is tainted with the nastiness of sin.

Of course, our Friday nights still came around and Lila would always watch the window to see us arrive. Whenever we walked through the door, we would see her running through the kitchen to greet us with her hugs, screaming my name. I remember teaching her my name and wondering if she would grasp who I was. I made a little game where we would sit on the couch, or play on the floor, and I would point to her and say, "Lila Kate," and then point at myself and say, "Allie." At times, I would get her hands and she would do it with me, or sometimes I would see how fast we could go, which resulted in endless laughs. Laughter was nonstop during my playdates with Lila.

She was the typical toddler who didn't sit still for two minutes! Except when it came to the famous "Let it go" song with toilet training, or sitting down to read the same book multiple times! Reading books was still our all-time favorite activity to do together and required! We would take turns reading our version of the book, usually multiple times, and in various fun voices. Looking back at our time together now, feels like one of our favorite books that was just one day shut. But, I keep reading it again, laughing, and getting the feels all the way through, knowing that God will use these little adventures to somehow point to his bigger adventure of unending grace, love, and goodness.

# ADVENTURE #5 – ONE OF THOSE DAYS

It was one of those days when it felt like the clock literally should've stopped, but it didn't. It was one of those days where typically I would've been excited for Friday, but I wasn't. It was one of those days the sun was *oh so bright* everywhere, except here, emotionally. It was one of those days that still makes me ill. The day was January 9, 2015.

I was about one week into my second semester of my senior year of high school; I had my mind set on graduation, and was wondering what adventure might unfold next. The world was at my fingertips, as I and most other graduates thought. The excitement and the uncertainty all mixed together with what might happen after high school. Little did we know what actually laid around the corner, and it was not the adventure I had in mind. However, it's the adventure God laid out, and that's the truth I have to choose to rest in daily. It's the adventure of the most devastating emotional pain I've ever felt. It's the adventure of the mind boggling undeserved grace that I've been given in my weakness, which always leads me back to the gospel. It's an adventure of the uncomfortable, while being continually reminded of the comfort one can find in Christ. Also, in other souls who He purposefully places along the way, usually in unique ways. That's why I choose to share. Maybe along the way God will use these adventures to comfort another hurting heart somewhere. When I first started writing, it was simply to capture my memories, but as I did so, I quickly began to see that God would use this as a tool to navigate my lifelong grieving process. As well as provide me with a platform to share my memories, and voice my mustard seed faith in the midst of such profound heartache.

January 2015, Lila Kate had been in the hospital for a few days with pneumonia, which was common with her health conditions, but it was also as if God said this is going to be the last time these little lungs have to battle any infections. It was a double whammy for LK this time, because she wasn't only fighting the pneumonia, but several other infections that had slithered into her already compromised immune system. I'm not sure why we didn't go visit her in the hospital. I've played with that question, along with many others, throughout the years, and I've drawn my temporary conclusion that maybe God wanted to leave me with a happy LK memory. In not going to the hospital, maybe God was protecting me in the process. I don't know, but I do know that my last LK memory was made just weeks before Christmas break.

LK made the *nice list* again and was ready to show me her new twin dolls and their stroller, though the dolls didn't captivate her as much as her new play kitchen did. She took great delight in her kitchen, feeding her dolls, and making felt food plates. On this particular day, I was able to play longer than usual, because school was out, and I was sitting at the kitchen table eating lunch, but LK didn't want me to take a break from playing, and she was adamant about not leaving me alone until I gave her my full attention. Yes, she was the typical toddler who loved every ounce of attention. While she was usually quite good at playing independently, this particular day was different. Now I'm thankful that I left my unfinished snack on the table. I figured it would become a dog snack, but after I came back, there was my food waiting on me.

# ADVENTURE #6 – THE GREATEST IS LOVE

God used Lila to teach me that not only does your best friend not have to be the same age as you, they also don't have to have the same number of chromosomes as you. God used Lila to show me and others more of His love. Her unexpected and unwanted entry to Heaven, became my personal, but not private, entry to a whirlwind of profound grief I'd never experienced before. I would never choose to go down this gray and clouded journey, but in almost the same breath, tiny peeks of sunshine have been given to me along the journey. Which were all unexpected blessings. The gray clouds won't vanish until that unclouded day mentioned in the old hymn, but until then I can continue to cling to the unwavering truth of God's words, and surround myself with others who will help me do the same.

I still recall the text quoted at LK's celebration of life; 1 Corinthians 13:7-13. When looking at the text in context, I see that it's the marching orders for the church, specifically the church in Corinth as they were straying from God's love, and that so affected how they loved one another. As a result, Paul encouraged the church to love as they have been loved, and pointed out that what we see with our human eyes is not always what's there. I know, it's a big thought and I'm not expanding outside of this text, because it can be a full Bible study, but in essence, Paul reminds his readers that we can't see the full picture. For me personally, I learned how to be thankful for such, because if this were the full picture, then I'd be looking for a different artist. But, no, I can attempt to rest in the truth of one day seeing how every little puzzle piece fits. Yes, right now, I only see in part, but one day I shall see fully. Until then, keep loving! For love is the greatest commandment, as Paul points out in almost all his letters. We can spend our days doing grand things for others, but if there's no love as the main ingredient, then it's pointless. We can spend our days doing the smallest things for others, and if that main ingredient is in the mixture, then even that smallest thing is worth it. The popular line comes to mind, "Do small things with great love," all the while resting in the truth that Christ already completed his work upon the cross with the resurrection, which restored our relationship with Him.

# ADVENTURE #7 – WRITE, WRITE, WRITE

I absolutely love getting new notebooks, but I love them more when a personal note is included. The notebook I happened to grab when LK went running up ahead to Heaven had the words "write, write, write" plastered on it, with a small but powerful note included from my cousin Lesley. Little did I know how much those words could actually summarize what I've attempted to do during these last six, almost soul crushing, years without LK!

*"Allie, girl! Keep your eyes upon God and my advice is to write, write, and write! You will love going back and seeing the blessings and answered prayers!"*

Quickly after Lila started exploring Heaven, I started exploring writing. Starting out, it was the tool that God used for me to best capture my priceless memories. So, "LK

Adventures," as one once called my social media posts, consisted of a beautiful LK memory. I might tie in a timely devotional thought or a Bible verse that I was holding close to my heart, along with a LK smile. I realized God was still using Lila to bring a smile to others' faces. He was doing it in a much different way than any of us wanted or expected, but He was and is still doing so even today.

As time progressed, so did my writing. God showed me that writing could be one of the multiple tools He would use to help me sort out my whirlwind of tough emotions. Actually, writing was the first way I expressed my big sadness as well as my mustard seed faith. Yes, together. I found through writing that I could process my raw emotions, and declare my tried faith. Writing was the first tool, which God used to help heal my heart, and a tool He continues to use. Of course, this took time, and I still get caught off guard occasionally with sticky emotions. In fact, I think we all do at some point on our journeys. And I even have seasons where I slip into a depression period, or *funky monkeys*, as I like to call them. Yet God remains faithful, and that truth alone changes the way I face these types of struggles.

Through writing God reminds me of not only my LK memories, but more importantly of His unchanging truth, which brings both comfort and refreshment to my heart. It seemed like everyone fell in love with LK all over again when they scrolled through my feed, and others encouraged me to write a book one day. God used my writing not only to bring comfort and refreshment to my heart, but to others as well. So, any opportunity for that, I don't want to delay.

However, I did delay for quite some time as I've shared previously. The whole thought of a book sounded farfetched, but it wasn't an idea that I totally disregarded either. I knew if God wanted me to write a book, then I needed to keep writing, and let Him place all the pieces together as I placed the letters together.

So "Play date," were the first of many words that God allowed me to capture, and even today when I read back over these words it results in more laughs and even more *heart tears*! I say *heart tears* because it's personally hard for me to cry just a little bit. When I cry, it's usually a big cry because I have limited self-control especially in this area! Today as I read through writings such as "Play date", I have a better understanding of this life not being the end and heaven is really just the beginning. Therefore, there's no need to change the ending.

## Playdates (February 2015)

*To find the correct words to write, to explain how much I miss Lila Kate is a useless task. It has been the worst experience, but it all came from the best experience I've had so far. I can play over and over the day we went to go meet Lila Kate. I had no idea that she would be my best friend! I look back and see that God opened that door for our friendship when she wasn't even born yet! Being the last student in the car rider line had its perks, I suppose.*

*LK and I kicked our friendship off perfectly! We would spend countless hours playing on the oversized blanket in the front room, reading and laughing. We also went outside when Skip permitted and the weather was nice. We didn't want her getting sick, which was easy for her to do, because of her low immune system. Lila Kate loved going outside and swinging high in her pink swing.*

*As the years flew by, Misty began to wonder when LK would start walking and talking. Of course, with more time, LK not only walked, ran to greet me when I came over, yelling, "Ollie, Ollie." We would always read together! I would read my version and then Lila would read her version to me. The endings were both usually very different even in the same book!*

*Today has been 5 weeks without being physically with LK. I want her back. If I could, I would change the ending to these words.*

Capturing these *virtual play dates* with LK on paper makes me feel like I'm spending time playing with her again, but when the memory ends, or the words stop coming, then I'm again reminded of the bitter truth of her absence. Here are a handful of the first memories with Lila Kate that I recorded in my notebook:

New shoes

*Baby steps. LK started walking when she was about three years old. Like the typical toddler, the floor swept her off her feet from time to time and we would have to help her get back up to her feet. She took small steps. Once she was steady, she tried walking with shoes, which always came off in the car, by her doing. Anyway, with the new shoes came a new challenge, because she didn't like the shoes. She would literally just stand there for a moment unsure why her feet were different!*

Potty time

*It was a joint effort to potty train LK. Elmo and Elsa both helped. Whoever might've been hanging with LK at the time, would periodically ask if she needed to use the bathroom. Usually, the automatic response was "no," so sometimes we would just move the party to the bathroom with Elmo or Elsa on the IPad. Elmo has a potty training app with all the steps of using the bathroom, and the song "Let It Go" from Frozen seems like the most appropriate toilet training song!*

One more cookie!

*LK loved her mini chocolate chip cookies and indeed the cookies loved her, too! Especially when she picked them before the main meal, which happened regularly. She was queen of the cookie eating business.*

Learning my name!

*When Lila and I started having regular playdates, I wondered if she would ever learn my name, and if she would recognize who I was when I came to play. In fact, I remember teaching her my name, because I made a game of it. I would point to her and say "Lila Kate," and then point to myself and say, "Allie." I would be silly, and at times go fast, which resulted in laughs. "Ollie, Ollie" indeed became words that were vocalized when her Daddy told her that I was coming home with her mommy that day. She would watch the window and knew I was there to play!*

# ADVENTURE #8 – EARLY ON IN MY GRIEF JOURNEY

As my reader knows, 2015 clearly kicked off with the unwanted. At the same time, I was finishing up my second semester of my senior year of high school and afterwards became fully occupied with accomplishing my basics out at our community college. I didn't really accept what literally shattered before my eyes. It took probably a good two years for me to really absorb the physical absence of Lila Kate, and when I fully accepted the new reality, I no longer comprehended life in the same way anymore—nor will it ever.

The unfolding of my grief definitely took me by surprise because as shared above it was a handful of years later when my emotions totally caught me off guard and I didn't realize that could actually be the case. Sure everyone is different and even each experience of dealing with losing a loved one can be different, but still I didn't have any similar experiences to relate to. Upon high school graduation, I continued to work part time at the local physical therapy clinic, which was and continues to be a total blessing that I will share more about at the end of my book. But in a nutshell. So working at the clinic, school, and many other things kept me on my toes I didn't really have time to grieve well. Which was okay, I was clearly occupied with everything and anything. I was doing "busy" overtime, which I came to learn is a wonderful distraction from the hurt. In fact, I don't care for the word busy. It has become a word that can replace how someone is really actually doing. Yes, the truth is everyone is pretty much busy but learning how to take time and pause with each other is important, too. Even nowadays I catch myself wanting to be so busy that I don't have to face my emotions and while in my opinion it's not a healthy coping skill, it works wonders some days. Regardless, one must face the rush of emotions because there's not a warning sign which reads: emotional disaster ahead.

One aspect that kept me going early in this journey was the children at church, in fact they still do! God always had a way of keeping my heart close to His, and early in this journey, I reflected on knowing that God used the smallest instruments in keeping me close to Him. With my healthy church background, my family could always be found being active members within our church family and we were excited to be a part of reaching others with the gospel, helping others, and serving others. It was actually through the church that I clearly found my gift of working with the small hearts and I was given the opportunity to teach Sunday school and volunteer with various activities. While this goes back to really a handful of years before 2015, I think it's something that God has clearly used and continues to use to keep my heart open, especially after experiencing having Lila's heart torn away from me.

# ADVENTURE #9 – THE SMALLEST TOOLS

As stated in the previous adventure, early from the start God clearly used, and continues to use, the smallest hearts as a key instrument in keeping my heart open as well as keeping me in His word and yes, even in the church building some weeks. I have a handful of journal entries that shed light on the distance I tended to experience in this particular season in my relationship with Christ and how I would open those ancient words and that's basically all. I understand not every time one sits down with their open Bible it's not always "as sweet as honey" or the handful of other similes that David used to describe God's words and I think it's okay to experience such, but it's not okay to stay there. But basically, I felt like I was just repeatedly opening and closing my Bible and that was all. But the key was I kept doing it and more importantly God kept on my heart.

Let's face it, my favorite four-year-old child was basically torn from my reach so anytime I spent time with other kiddos my mind and my emotions went straight to my playdates with Lila that I no longer enjoyed on this side of living. Over time and with careful help from specific friends, I've learned how to change my perspective from overwhelming sadness to maybe a little joy. I've learned that's okay and doing so helps keep my memories fresh. I absolutely love children—in small doses—and I literally pour my heart into their wellbeing! As an example, a few weeks ago we had an Easter party with the kiddos at church where we did an egg hunt, packed blessing bags, made an edible craft, and of course shared the gospel. If LK was physically here, I would've taken her too and this thought was my focal point, of course. I did the evening with a smile and tons of laughs, but my heart was so upset. It was on a Friday and LK's 11th birthday was around the bend, so my emotions were already whacked up and unfortunately they came out in unhealthy ways which almost caused me not to go forth with the evening. But we did. I was planning to take a beautiful wild child along with us who was recently adopted by her foster parents. Doing this would give the parents a break and it would be like taking Lila with me. It was a win-win situation, I thought. This little girl was four years old and full of sassy love, just like Lila was! And that's exactly what this little girl reminded me of, in such a vivid way. That Lila Kate is still beautiful, still full of love, and even fuller of life now in Heaven! That is the thought I must daily rest upon and some days I do well with, and some days I don't, which has to be okay, too.

Flash back to 2016, which kicked off with my grandpa arriving at the golden gates and all the stuff that comes along with such an experience; and there was a blessing hidden in it for me. With all the family in from out of town, my aunt hooked up with a high school friend which we now call basically family: The Izors. At the time, Debbie Izor was looking for a part time caregiver for Jerron (her grandson) who would be starting Pre-K soon, and as it turned out, we would get the opportunity to fill that need. Jerron spent three to four nights a week with us and he sure added some eventfulness to our afternoons and evenings. He and I quickly hit it off well together; we did homework, played, and enjoyed bedtime reading together. It was a family affair taking him to ball practices or the occasional birthday parties on the weekend, but during the season he was with us he definitely kept me on my toes and my heart open for love. The timing of our paths crossing was an absolute "God-timing." Jerron's Daddy saw Heaven basically on Jerron's first day of school. The tragedy was great for this family, specifically this mother who had seen two boys go to Heaven already. God used this family and their pain to touch my heart in a way that was just what I needed during this particular season.

Another small heart that was used early upon this journey was another little girl in foster care who is now adopted. Almost immediately after the McAlister family was forced to depart physically from Lila, Misty decided it was their turn to have the experience of serving as a foster family. They had a handful of kiddos come and go from their home, but there was one who had a life changing impact on me, for the better. She totally reminded everyone of LK. She was three or four years old, and she quickly grew on me and we indeed became friends quickly! My LK memories surfaced every time we were together and it was emotionally challenging, but totally worth loving on another little life. My mom and I would help out in any way possible as we babysat regularly, picked her up from daycare, and even took her to church with us sometimes. She greeted everyone with hugs and her shoes escaped her feet when she got in the car, very similar to LK! During this season God really showed me how walking with someone else in pain, just might be what He is using to help me with my aches, too.

Even in this current season as I'm finishing up the first edit of my book, I see God still using small hearts to aid in my healing, specifically babies and toddlers in foster care. Not too long ago, God crossed our paths with yet another child who was totally what I needed at the time and she needed us, too! She was eighteen months old when we met her, and she expressed those same belly laughs that LK used to make! She had that lizard tongue, too, and also took her shoes off in the car like LK usually did! Indeed, I shared an unusual friendship with her and we bonded in ways that neither I nor my family usually get to with children in foster care. This opportunity was very unique to us and so we wanted to do something a little unique for her foster parents, so we gave them a swing for the little girl to use, and I attached this note to the foster parents:

*Reagan and Jansen,*                                                    *July 2021*

*I don't think God could've picked a more special foster home for baby G! Each healthy home is special, but this go around has been most special to me! Besides being y'all's first go around on being an "open home" and our first time to do a transition between homes, there's something that makes this even more special! Baby G is the spitting image of my best friend, LK (picture below), who went to live in Heaven at too young of an age. LK had a spunky personality and she was full of light with love for all to see! Similar to Baby G.*

*We wanted to get Baby G a swing because first I figured she would belly laugh as she was pushed, but then secondly LK LOVED her swing!! It brings me heart smiles to see Baby G laugh, because it reminds me that LK is probably laughing in Heaven and we can laugh regardless of the tough patches in the past…baby G is good at that, too!!*

*Love you guys,*

*Allie*

As it turns out, God did something big and very unique, too! This still gives me chills and reminds me that God can use such random ways to remind us of His presence especially in pain! In response to this note I sent, I received the following text message:

*Just wanted to share a crazy way that God works! I just read your SWEET card that brought me to tears!! Lila Kate was actually the cousin of one of my dear friends from college, Rebekah Holliman. I actually went to her "LK 5K" the first year they held it! It is so special to me that you got to know and love her and form a sweet bond with her. Thankful G gets to bring you back some sweet memories of her! We are so thankful for you guys and G couldn't have had a better family to spend her transition time with! I can't wait for her to try out her new swing!*

## Adventure #10 - Grief Unfolding

Back on the timeline. The summer of 2017 was a turning point for me, for worse, unfortunately. At that moment, summer knocked me off my toes completely and my journal entries reflected my extreme roller coaster of emotions. From my frequent journal entries and shared posts, I didn't sound like the upbeat, positive, happy-go-lucky person that I knew and I didn't quite know why. One particular Sunday during our typical prayer meeting during lunch, our pastor made a request to pray for those within our church family who had lost a family member and to pray for them even after the initial loss. BINGO, a giant sized lightbulb sparked, but thankfully the word didn't race out of my mouth! I obviously recalled being "slow to speak," as James commands in James 1:19, but with that prayer request it was as if God was confirming why I'd been feeling this big heaviness that was pounding in my chest day after day.

At the same time that I was beginning to realize this unexpected emotional heaviness, guess what my family was planning, yes a trip. Of course, my family was planning a trip. It seems like we are always talking about where to go next and this time it was Seattle for my cousin's wedding. Someone (me) didn't really want to go and the airport was the most memorable experience in a negative way. Airports are not my favorite anyway, but this time everything got the best of me. To the point where even the security guard was worried about me! I was simply in emotional overload and I just was beginning to realize it.

When we returned home, my family jumped back into typical day-to-day schedules. I may have jumped in physically, but not emotionally or mentally. I was still experiencing these unexpected and frequent emotional highs and lows. I decided to reach out to our pastor for he had told me that I could talk to him if I wanted, so I did. Asking for help can be a challenge for anyone, especially if it's regarding old hurts, and personally, I don't like to be a burden on anyone. But I've learned that it's healthy to ask for help and we are called to share each other's burdens, as Paul reminds us in Galatians 6:2. As I began to attempt to sort out my emotions with him, I gathered that I was up against Depression and who would've ever guessed? Not this girl! Yet, this was the start of what I call those "funky monkeys," otherwise known as specific periods when I experienced a state of Depression. This was a huge important lesson to learn: I was not depressed, but I was experiencing states of Depression, and I still do from time to time. And that's okay. I use those specific words because it's so important how one talks to oneself, regardless of Depression or not. The word on the streets is that self is the person we listen to the most, and it's especially important when it involves big conversations such as Depression. It's scary. It's easy to lose the identity of ourselves or even others based on the label of an illness or condition, yet it's important to know what's really going on, so one must label these things without letting that label become one's identity. As a child of God, I believe my identity rests in Him ... even when I'm in a depressed state. My identity in Christ never changes! I'm still loved! I'm still chosen! And so are you!

These are a handful of notebook entries which were noted during this particular season:

*Idk. I just don't feel right. I can't pinpoint how I feel; it just doesn't feel right. It doesn't feel right because LK is not here and she's not coming back. God refreshes me a bit through His words. His words are life because He is Life. I have life through His Name. I know God wants and deserves my whole heart, even when it's hurting. Idk but I do know everywhere there's a reminder of summer without my BFF.*

*I have been struggling with too many unpleasant emotions these last few weeks, but Christ struggled too. He struggled more. He struggled for me. And now because He has struggled, I don't struggle alone. And plus, after Christ struggled, He experienced and is experiencing endless glory—which He promises to me too, after I struggle.*

*I hurt. I'm hurting. I'm hurt. Whatever the correct usage may be, maybe upon this entry, my aching heart hurts. I'm ready for Heaven, but God is still preparing me.*

*My heart is cold, but just how the sun can warm my body ... the Son can warm my heart through His words. He is still my comfort and sometimes His comfort is clearly seen through others.*

As we were in Seattle I shared the following;

*My current situation: I'm sitting in my hotel room, alone. It's early afternoon and I just showered to get back in my PJ's. Is that disheartening? Not according to me, I actually feel the best I've felt all day. I've had a full morning with cousins and The Art Museum. So let's catch up, Dad flew us to Seattle for my cousin's wedding. I despised the idea of traveling when I was preparing for this trip. I tend to enjoy traveling but this trip I didn't want to go forth! The whole airplane travel process, being away from my house, being around lots of new people, and packing a bag for four full nights when one might be having a difficult time picking out the outfit for one given day. That's not me at all. All throughout this past month; I haven't been my free, bubbly and cheerful self. I blame it on grief with the rush of emotions which can come out of nowhere. I'm positive that's the culprit.*

*My description of self is the heaviness of the hurt has been too much...the emptiness of my heart has been too much, (I know only God can fill those empty spots), the ache that never leaves and it seems to only gets worse (it seems) and the tug that tells my heart that I get the grand privilege of living the rest of my life on earth, only without my best friend. And there's my run on sentence, which I'm confident breaks all the possible grammar rules.*

*But here I sit glancing over the city of Tacoma; watching the boats come in and out of the harbor, hearing the traffic of the town down below, and shaming on grief and/or Depression or whatever I'm feeling. I'm not too sure. I realize the weight, the emptiness, and the tug can't and shouldn't be ignored. But I'm unsure how to deal with such; especially with a smile.*

# ADVENTURE #11 – INFLATABLE TUBE MAN/ "AFTERSHOCKS"

During this particular season, I can say I was beginning to experience the "aftershocks" of Lila's homecoming. I was totally preoccupied with Lila Kate's physical absence and every free moment I had invited more time for my heavy emotions to overwhelm me, therefore I was again continually busy. I honestly felt like I was going through the motions of life, from everything to Bible studies to school. I was like the inflatable tube man that you see at car dealerships, that wacky, waving advertising man, raising and falling with each swish of the wind. I understand that life is full of mountains and valleys, but this experience with my tough emotions was all new to me. My highs and lows were a bit extreme. I'd never experienced such waves of emotions before. Everything continued when it felt like life should simply stop; or that's how I felt periodically.

Our pastor and I shared frequent email conversations as he continually encouraged me by reminding me of God's unchanging truth and God's unchanging love, which were the exact reminders my heart needed. Our pastor also reassured me that he was there for me, which was the biggest blessing, and even in the years since that time he continues to show me such care. To this day he's a special blessing to me.

This particular year for Christmas, I wanted a Sunday school room makeover! The room still looked the same from when I was a little girl and was in major need of some bright colors. So apparently I made the cut for the "nice list" and the little elves devoted several weekends before Christmas to completing this project. While working on the project one afternoon, I made an escape. I obviously wasn't helping much, so I decided to pay our pastor a visit to his office. The first of many. I was nervous, but I also knew that sharing verbally was another healthy step for me to take on my healing journey.

Surprisingly, around this same time, I was determined to kick off 2018 with excitement, so I decided to go to Costa Rica! Yes! This was pretty much my choice and my dad went along with me, because there was no way my parents were letting me leave the country without them. And thank goodness, this time the airport experience was a lot smoother. I simply wanted to escape from everything, including my hard emotions. I know running from the hard stuff is not always the thing to do, but our church already had a group planning to go and when they opened it up for others to go, I was definitely going!

For years, we'd shared a partnership with a local missionary there and supported them throughout the process of planting a church. This particular trip was a celebration of the work God has done, as well as looking forward to what He will continue to do in Costa Rica. The trip was definitely a first for me, because it was also my first time being out of the country. It was refreshing to me to have a change of scenery, to explore, and to see the fulfillment of God's work in Costa Rica.

During this same time, I noted the following:

*Reflecting over these last few months, I've seen my grief unravel. Since LK's passing, there have been numerous situations to occupy my empty space. Whether it be excitement for starting college or others' illnesses that I was concerned about ... grief didn't consume me. As God's child, I do realize He is the only one that can fill any emptiness and He desires for me to be consumed with an eternal focus. This I fail at daily, because I'm human. Yet God still chooses me! Nonetheless I have experienced the "grief roller-coaster" at full speed, so no wonder at times I feel knots in my stomach, and spinning, paralyzing thoughts. It's up, down, backwards, forwards, and possibly upside down! But I'm still fascinated with the goodness of God. Yes, God is continually good to this broken heart. Since no one can see God on earth, it's up to those of us who believe in Him to show Him to others. And that's exactly what stands out the most during this emotional rollercoaster ride, the physical hands that come alongside me simply to love me; and to be able to see Jesus' hands in the midst of it all, the hands that were nailed for me and for you.*

# Adventure #12 – A Special Tool of Investing

During this particular season, God was starting to use our pastor, Jeff Hill, to be a very special tool in my life. He was the first person I remember verbally sharing LK with from an emotional standpoint. I'll always be thankful for the time he invested in me. Sometimes time is the best gift because it's non-refundable. The time one spends with a person can show how much one cares and this was the biggest blessing our pastor gave me during this season: time and simply being there. He obviously noted how Job's friends sat with him during his profound grief experience. During our weekly conversations, he would provide me a safe place to share my emotions without judgment. He would bring scripture into our conversations but he would never be pushy with it. He would challenge me to think about things with a new outlook. As an example, "think about how much you enjoyed your friendship with LK on Earth where sin still does exist. And now think about how much more you will enjoy your friendship with LK in heaven where sin does not exist."

Eventually, our pastor and I started sharing books together as I was aware of my dad doing so with a friend of his, and I suppose I thought maybe I could, too! So I asked our pastor about doing so and he agreed. We would complete a weekly reading, and that reading would be the topic of discussion the following week. Our pastor is the one for me to thank for turning me into a bookworm! I found that reading books helped me tremendously, because they served as an escape for me, but these certain books were also showing me different perspectives on Scripture and grief. Even today, I'm usually continually reading a book. My favorite book our pastor as yet to share with me is called *Not God Enough by J.D Greear*, as it shares countless insights of the limited perspective we sometimes place on our limitless God. The author suggests we have learned to put God in a box and in doing so, have given Him boundaries that he doesn't really have. It's a book packed with imagery so it's easier to remember for most minds and I've referenced it several times throughout my book.

As I previously stated, the biggest blessing that God gave me through our pastor was that he simply showed me that he cared. Yes, I knew my parents cared, but sometimes randomly bringing grief up in conversation was difficult. It could be difficult in a counseling visit, too, but these visits were integral in my healing. I was given a specific time and a specific person to share with. There's nothing wrong with healthy counseling and it's so important. Actually throughout the process of writing this book, I was re-connected with another special heart who has shared weekly visits during this current season of my life. I'll share more in Part III but I can say my visits with him bring so much refreshment to my heart and I'm so thankful God provided me with this relationship.

And yes, I know God cares, but sometimes God's "caring" is shown through people who He allows to cross one's path! Similar to when God called Moses, as it's noted in Exodus 2:24-25, God heard, saw, and knew about the Israelites' sufferings, so what did God do? He called Moses and obviously Moses was one of the few who had "Caller ID" back then because Moses didn't really want to answer the call. But he did, along with the help of Aaron; so see sometimes it's not one specific person who God uses for one specific assignment! I'm not saying one might need five different counseling sessions with five different people, but I am saying each person God allows to cross our paths is probably there for a specific reason and can bring a different perspective. God has a way of timely crossing's paths with people who we might need to speak words of life into us, to remind us of the truth, and to be there simply to listen during specific seasons. Sometimes different seasons mean different people, and that's okay! We must not dismiss the fact of God working through His children! He has special assignments for each of us and we have an unknown due date, so that's why it's important to be in step with Him—always looking for opportunities to better others, to serve others, and to love others. Not too long ago our pastor's sermon was: I can spend my life investing in my kingdom which will fade quickly, or I can spend my life investing in His lasting kingdom. When I invest in His kingdom that means I'm part of investing in others in the hopes that if they don't know Christ, they'll come to know Him. And if they do know Christ, then I'm investing with the hope that they'll come to know Him better. That was the sermon in probably three sentences (wink, wink). It's almost like a cause and effect type deal because, when one intentionally helps another get to know Christ better, then it's almost an automatic effect that he or she will come to know Christ better, too!

Each of us can continually get to know Christ better, even as Paul did. He's one of the top New Testament writers, and he wrote Philippians, one of my favorite books! And maybe Paul in general is one of my favorites. The transforming grace which is clearly seen in his life and his calling is of note to be an example for all of God's kiddos. But here in Philippians, from a jail cell, writing his letter to the church in Philippi he made his goal clear: "I press on toward the goal for the prize of the upward call of God in Christ Jesus," (Philippians 3:14). Paul was continually focused on his personal walk with the Lord because he realized his personal growth with Christ was an ongoing lifelong transformation. But too, Paul was mindful of investing in others and by doing so, he was investing in the gospel.

Oftentimes, Paul's letter to the Phillipians is summarized by the single word of joy, and while this is true I also see sorrow. In truth, "sorrow upon sorrow," as mentioned in Philippians 2:27. For Paul, there were people back home who were physically sick and in one intense moment Paul basically says, "if this guy gets better and goes to Heaven then I'll have sorrow upon sorrow!" Not simply sorrow, but "sorrow upon sorrow!" Now this was Paul, who actually understood the vastness of Heaven and still if he sees his buddy go to Heaven, he says he'll experience such sorrow. When I heard this in a similar comment pointed out by Levi Leskso, who's an incredible pastor, writer, and seemingly an incredible family guy, God used this truth to comfort my heart very much. Even to this day, it's a truth that hits home, especially on days where I'm hurting too much!

From what I can gather, we are His vessels; He delights in choosing us to carry out His plan. He chooses us not because He is dependent upon us (far from it) but He chooses us because He loves us! He created us to be fully dependent upon Him, but not independent of others.

# Adventure #13 – Hurting and Hurting Some More

Back on the timeline. Even though I was attempting to move forward, it was just another step to endure, and really the beginning of my grief unfolding. My journal entries reflected the many "funky monkeys" I was experiencing. I felt completely overwhelmed with my grief. I could tell I was dealing with Depression; which is definitely something that doesn't match my personality normally. Depression is not simply sadness; it can look different on everyone. In my experience, it's an awkward heaviness that I can literally wake up with. At first I was extremely hard on myself and didn't know quite how to handle such. I just wanted to feel better. But with time and specific hearts I have learned how to handle my lows so much better! Depression can come in all kinds of shapes and forms. It's not one size fits all. I warn my reader to be careful reading the following because I don't want to throw out more misconceptions about Depression. Right here I'm just sharing my experience with one of my "funky monkeys" that was apparently too funky at the time.

During the summer of 2019, I bottomed out on the "lows" and experienced very challenging thoughts. The famous grief roller coaster felt more like a downward spiral. My heart and body were exhausted from hurting. I simply wanted Heaven, now, and not later. Obviously and thankfully, it came up one week when visiting our pastor and eventually I was able to share. The hardest action was sharing. It wasn't necessarily that I wanted to kill myself but I definitely wanted to die; yes, there's a difference. I made comments along the lines of "If I could go to Heaven without anyone knowing, I would book the first flight." I won't say I was completely suicidal, because I could control my thoughts quite well but I was overwhelmed with my pain and I wanted a escape.

Sure a healthy desire for Heaven is simply that, healthy. I see the concept over and over in Scripture with the writings of David, Paul, and maybe others. But there is a balance and let's say that the seesaw wasn't balancing that well. David had an increased desire for Heaven when his child died, in 2 Samuel 12, but all the while he continued living out God's calling upon his life. The response to David's child entering Heaven is completely opposite thinking to me sometimes and challenges me even to this day! David's response to such distress challenges me because it was right after the baby entered Heaven when David basically cheered up! He washed, ate, and went back to living his life. While the baby was sick, David was strongly discouraged and showed physical signs of Depression. Even in many of the Psalms I see David's desire for Heaven, especially when he's troubled, but then he recalls that God is surrounding him here, too; and he continues to go forth. For us to have a God who welcomes our hurts, and actually hurts with us, is something noteworthy of praise! I also want to note this description of the Psalms from Michael R. Emlet: "The psalms of lament don't ... read like this: 'Since I've finally resolved all my anger and doubts and grief in private, now I can publicly recount God's faithfulness and purposes in the midst of suffering.' No, in many psalms the honest wrestling plays out right before our eyes (and the eyes of God). It's encouraging that God models patience in listening to his people's cries, tears, questions, and doubts."

Then there's Paul, who uses phrases such as "groaning" and "eager longing" (Romans 8:19-22) to describe his yearning for Heaven, but he also knew there were people on earth to whom he had the ability to show God's hand. He knew that his body was an earthly tent (2 Corinthians 5:1) which God would take down one day and he was basically on a camping trip as a traveler upon this world. Even Paul describes some of his "adventures" as "burdened beyond our strength" and "despaired life itself," but Paul tells his reader why this was and it was for the reason "...to make us rely not on ourselves but on God who raises the dead." (2 Corinthians 1:9) And to note here, I clearly see what Paul was writing about when he writes: "Blessed be the God and Father of our Lord Jesus Christ, the Father of mercies and God of all comfort, who comforts us in all our affliction, so that we may be able to comfort those who are in any affliction, with the comfort with which we ourselves are comforted by God." (2 Corinthians 1:3-4). I absolutely am amazed at how God can intersect people's paths and do something too cool, and hopefully my reader has seen that throughout my book.

One more example, Elijah's desire for Heaven, but his was a bit too deep. In 1 Kings 19, he literally asked God to physically take his life away, because it was too much. In response, God refreshed Elijah by physical rest, a touch, and a meal. The angel who touched him actually agreed that the journey was too much for Elijah, and I've learned from personal experience that having someone come alongside you and agree that this is tough stuff makes a huge difference. As it did for Elijah, he had a talk with God and was carried along. As he went forward, he found Elisha and together they assisted each other. And that's the point, as I reflect on this three years later, I'm beyond ecstatic that those scary thoughts didn't get the best of me. I can't say these scary thoughts don't ever creep up on me anymore. In fact they did as I was finishing up this book, but I understand that everyone has ups and downs, and with time hopefully one learns how to cope with all this stuff that life throws at all of us in one way or another. And not simply coping, but rising above the hurt and somehow letting it be the very instrument to do what only God can do!

These are a handful of notebook entries which were noted during this particular season:

*My emotions and thoughts are so mixed today. Today is the 9th. Lila went to Heaven on the 9th. It's August, I know it's so strange. But it's Friday and January 9th, 2015 was a Friday. Complicated. Jesus too died on a Friday, but that wasn't the end of the story."*

*God allows me to choose joy daily. In fact, He commands such through Paul's letter of Philippians. The fact that Jesus chooses me and loves me fills me with joy, which I hope to choose daily. And even when I fall short of choosing joy, He still chooses me! Because He's simply that good.*

*Lots of "whys," but Jesus asked "why," too. When I reflect on His "why," I realize He meets me in my pain and also places others in my path to help me navigate these waters. I'm thankful.*

## (Partial) Suicide Awareness (Summer 2017)

*I was encouraged "to bring thoughts out of the darkness of my mind and into the light of God and certain people." Those were our pastor's words to me and how perfectly those words fit into this book, even though at the given time the words were almost crippling to hear and act upon! At the time, we were getting ready to welcome family into town. Everyone was excited but everywhere around was the visible image of summer without my best friend! I was nowhere near myself. I was acting bubbly and cheerful on the outside, but on the inside I wanted to flee. I wanted to flee from myself. I can't say I was suicidal all the way but I can say I wanted Heaven on every degree possible. I was exhausted physically, emotionally, and probably spiritually, too. My grief felt like a downward spiral I couldn't escape. I was depleted.*

*I wanted Heaven and my patience was failing. I didn't experience self harm thoughts, but I would occasionally wish "something bad" might happen that would kill me. These thoughts were very confusing to me and then to share was even more confusing. But God was and is still timely about surrounding me with just the right person to help me at my low points. At my lowest of lows, I was dead in my sin and God provided Christ. A person. A person who died so I could live not only right now but in eternity. Heaven is ready when He says so, not when I say so.*

*Recently these thoughts came sneaking up on me again for that is what Satan does best; he's sneaky with his ways. And again I went through the process of sharing, which was much easier this go round. God provided exactly the right people who are so good at being good! And plus the book which I happened to be reading through was a giant ole "God wink" for the words in the current chapter describing the exact same experience I was having! One section reads: "When dark thoughts come, when you feel like giving up, make a conscious choice to counter these lies with what God says, with His truth. Give yourself the opportunity to stay in the fight." (Jennie Lusko)*

*I never want to dismiss the need for medical help in experiencing Depression or suicidal symptoms for there is absolutely a time and place for such, but it's not every time nor in every place! God has given doctors to mankind, and sometimes they may be exactly the tool that He uses to get His child through this scary process! There's a weird stigma out there as far as suicide goes, people tend to judge the person or even the family members! The person didn't give up; these harmful thoughts are challenging to work through and the enemy easily uses them for his benefit. These thoughts aren't easily shared so they can be easily hidden from family or friends; so simply keep showing up for people who have experienced grief of any type.*

# Adventure #14 – An Unexpected Blessing

I tend to find random quotes and I thought the following could be placed here because it's fleshed out so perfectly when I reflect on how Cody crossed my path. It's a quote by Lindsey Wheeler and it reads;: "No matter what kind of pain a person is suffering, parts of that pain are universal. Whether it's emotional pain from loss or disappointment, or physical pain from illness or injury, everyone in pain has something in common with others. One of the unexpected gifts of facing great pain in my own life has been learning to recognize my fellow travelers in this journey of suffering and sharing comfort in the sheer knowledge that we don't suffer alone."

One Sunday evening, this particular person who I barely knew actually made my eyes leak during his testimony. I'm usually not like that and I usually laugh at the serious moments, which often results in me camping out in the back where I can escape if needed. The worst is during the Lord's supper while holding the world's tiniest cup without spilling. But anyway, this particular night God used this young guy's testimony to plant a seed which I wouldn't see until a little later, when it blossomed into a friendship that would mean so much to me.

So yes, God has a way of taking small encounters and doing something big with them. His timing is always worth the wait because it's perfect. Never underestimate what God can do in and through ugliness. I think He's always doing something within a believer's heart to build them or someone else up, and bring them closer to Christ. What God does in one person's life is never solely just with the one person in mind. You might not always see that play out, especially in the midst of pain, but reflecting back is humbling. And as Cody still reminds me, we all go through "stuff" to help others go through "stuff," too. And he's right! We can allow God to use these ugly "funky monkeys" for His beautiful purposes as we reach out to Him as well as others. Or we can allow the devil to get his way and turn away from God as well as others. It's a daily choice and I don't choose God's way every day, as it's easier to give into my flesh. But as I lift my everything to God and surround myself with others who can gently help me do the same, then and only then I can do things through my pain which only He can do through me!

Cody was such a huge unexpected blessing during this particular season and if it wasn't for each of our personal's experiences with such profound grief I really don't know if we would share the unique friendship that we both cherish during this particular season. God has shown me that He usually has better than what we asked for. A wee bit before we started sharing a friendship, I simply asked God for someone to shed a little light upon their grief experience. Instead God gave me so much more than that; God gave me a friendship. Cody and I have been able to make countless, priceless memories together with my family around the dinner table. We are continually encouraging each other, and during some particular seasons God often used him to lift my spirits when I experienced a "funky monkey." I've thoroughly enjoyed watching our friendship bloom even if it's just for a season or so. Regardless, this friendship will be forever treasured by me, and Cody will always hold a special place in my heart.

# Adventure #15 – the halfway point ... I thought!

I originally thought this would be the famous halfway point in this book, but God had more. God always has more. He loves us more! Yes, my reader probably gathers that I take great delight in escaping to my "writing world" and as I've shared, writing has been the primary tool which I use to share God's goodness with others and to process my grief. But, I'm a bit on the scattered side especially when it comes to actually putting an actual book together. I was continually encouraged to go forth with a book but everytime I would attempt I would get too caught up in "the feels" and push my writings back under my bed. But when I remember it's not simply about me and what I can do, but what He can do in and through me, then I proceed with the task. And that thought has not only helped me in the writing life, but with life in general. It's encouragement from Cade Hill, who is a person I consider a treasure!

So originally when I started this book in August 2020, part I of the book was supposed to be a glimpse at the timeline from roughly the time that I met Lila Kate up until roughly the present. As I reflect upon these different seasons of life, I'm reminded of one truth that is the same and will always be the same, the evidence of God. Through all the high mountaintops and deep waters, God was and will be evident. For part II of the book, I'll be revisiting some of my journal entries from years past and shedding present light upon them. My journals have been a lifeline to me and while at times it's difficult to revisit some of those dark entries, it's also rewarding to me. I'll share with prayers that God will use them to stir the hearts of those who read them, for that somehow gives meaning to my mixture of hurts. Yes, with every fiber I still ache for Lila Kate to be back with me, but when God teaches me to shift my grief, I know that He will use everything in His greater adventure which is covered in love, grace, and simple goodness. And that's what this book is for, to share my story, but more importantly to point my reader to His greater story. That is my simple yet complex task.

After completing parts I and II, I thought I was done with my first book. I thought it was enough and it was, but like I said above, God tends to have more. This go around, He showed me that He has more by very unusual ways. Nonetheless I decided to attempt to be diligent with the task of daily journal entries, because I was basically in the habit of writing every day, and I would find myself going back into my book and changing words. While this can be healthy it can also be dangerous! I realized that I needed to be still and know that God has guided my fingers with each word, but to be still is not necessarily doing nothing. God doesn't often call His children to do nothing. Maybe there are a few instances, but when I hear the words "be still" I automatically reflect upon when God used Moses to part the Red Sea in Exodus 14. The command was there to be still, but at the same time Moses was instructed to step into the dry sea. So I decided, well I'm already in the sea and the waters are parted, so why not add a part III and continue to touch more coolness within the sea! There's a funny anecdote our pastor shares about the splitting of the Red Sea. He says he wonders if the people stuck their fingers into the sides of the water grasping for sea animals or whatnot.

So with part III, my reader will see I still struggle. But nonetheless, I want to allow God to daily take this hurt and use it to not only bring me closer to His heart but other hearts as well. So when they want to stop their pain, they won't; but instead maybe they'll be encouraged in some fashion that only God can encourage! He's the God of encouragement, according to Romans 15:5. Anyway, with 2020 and the word "quarantine" becoming a part of our unchosen vocabulary, I decided maybe it was the perfect opportunity to write more! The excuse "I don't have time" couldn't fly, because we were basically stuck at home for a handful of weeks during this time. I pulled out my old notebooks and lavished over them! I enjoyed reflecting on God's faithfulness and while our world was basically unsure; I felt sure. I've seen too much of God's faithfulness and goodness not to be sure. This is not to say that the time I spent reflecting wasn't emotionally challenging for me, but I can say I had an equal balance of grief and joy mixed together.

When quarantine orders were lifted, I continued to write. Thankfully! I'm horrible at starting something, then getting a new idea and leaving a project undone; which even happened during this go around, but I saved my work and maybe God will allow it to be used for another project later. Regardless, here I am! I always told myself if I simply kept typing the letters, God would open the doors to help me publish a work. In the early months of 2021, I thought I was pretty close to having enough for a book (parts I and II) and the idea of self-publishing was floating around my thoughts. During this time, I slipped into a funky monkey and reached out to one of my friends (who happens to be a pastor) to talk and through visiting, he encouraged me to start talking about my book more. I then informed him that I could start practicing with him and surprisingly he agreed. Nonetheless, I started looking for opportunities to share more with different people and one day when my mom was on the phone with her sister, the topic of Amazon came up and that triggered the thought of my book because I was leaning towards self-publishing on Amazon. As the conversation flowed, I was reminded that my cousin was an incredible, gifted, and heartfelt writer so maybe she could give me some pointers. Sure enough she did and little did she know that she was in for the long haul! The whole writing process was literally a walk in faith and again God showed me that He delights in working through different people!

# Part 2:

# Reflecting on Journal Entries from 2015 - 2020

# Adventure #16 – the HARDEST WORDS TO WRITE

January 4, 2015

*Lila Kate McAlisterMarch 31, 2010 - January 9, 2015. Those were the hardest words and numbers to place on paper. Thank you God for the four years I had with Lila Kate. That's all I can write.*

Even today as I copy this entry into my book, almost six years later, those are still the hardest, ugliest, and almost soul-crushing words (and numbers) I've ever penned on paper. As I'm typing this, it's literally one month until the date marks six years. As I might have shared before, the anticipation of these dates are the worst for me! At times, I still get lost for words. As a writer, that's not a good feeling to have. I reflect on this first journal entry that I recorded after LK ran to Heaven, and I'm amazed that one of the first aspects was that I thanked God for the little girl. I don't know about my reader, but thankfulness isn't usually the first thing that pops into my head as I'm hurting. Because usually on "those days," I tend to look for an escape for my pain instead of being thankful in the midst of such distress. But these are the first words that I recorded, and I'm amazed how God has used my journal entries to encourage my heart even today. I'm reminded of His goodness and faithfulness all along the way. It's my prayer that He does the same for my reader in a special way, as only He can do!

While those are still the hardest, ugliest, and almost soul-crushing words to write, they are and will always be the words that marked a beautiful beginning and a beautiful ending to a little life upon this earth. A life that was literally my best friendship yet. A life that was filled with unfailing love, hugs, and smiles. A life that was definitely shortened on Earth, but a life that God continues to use to be an instrument of His love and His goodness even along the dirty sin-stained paths that we each travel on our way home. And too, those words are the words that have shown my eyes the unchanging faithfulness and goodness of God.

# Adventure #17 – Too Much

March 4, 2015

*I'm angry. I'm past tired. It's more like I'm exhausted. It's too much mentally, emotionally, spiritually, and physically.*

Research has shown that anger is close to the first stage when facing the grieving process. I wasn't aware of this at the time, nor any other of the five stages of the grief process: denial, anger, bargaining, depression and acceptance. The grieving process is simply a tough process and one doesn't experience all five stages in a linear manner because one usually jumps back and forth between one stage to the other; or at least that's my experience. And too, there's really no set order for how one might experience these different stages. It can be a life-long process. But while it's tough, God can and will do tough with His children. He's right there, even in the tough stuff.

I was weeks away from high school graduation, and, yes, I

was the weird student who didn't want to leave high school. I literally had all my teachers, friends, and even the principal tied around my finger. Each year, I creatively found a way to grasp various teachers' classroom door keys, and I always made a pretty great escape from the chaos of the various drills that were "mandatory." Yes, I was a rebel. I even knew when my principal and the crew had lunch so I would pay them all a visit at least once a week in the cafeteria and was given the opportunity to be the "hallway monitor" because it seemed to them that I was in the hallway more than I was in class. Ruh-roh, yet they seemed cool about it. Actually, one year my classes were back to back at opposite ends of the building so I did have a lot of steps to fit into an entire school day.

After graduation, I had a plan of attending the local community college for my basics so it wasn't like I was clueless on what was next, but the whole new reality of Lila being in Heaven was a very fresh wound for me. I've noticed from some repetitive journal entries that I had drifted away in my Bible studies and had very little desire to spend time with God at that time. I confessed to God that my hunger wasn't there like it used to be. It for sure wasn't what David described in Psalms 42; "As a deer pants for flowing streams, so pants my soul for you, O God."

I was stagnant. I was dry. I was simply going through the motions. As I've learned, everyone is subjected to dry spells in their walk with Christ or simply with life in general. It's okay to be at those points, but it's not okay to stay at those points. To me, that's a fine line in many aspects of our lives.

# Adventure #18 – Dealing with Anger

June 1, 2015

*I miss Lila Kate more than words can say. I can't put these feelings into enough words. Yes, some days are good but most are not. I fall into pits of anger.*

I was clearly spinning with emotions and the most prominent one was anger. I wasn't necessarily angry at God. Sure, I didn't delight in the fact that Lila Kate was so far away, but the anger I felt was more towards myself. My personality is bubbly, cheerful, and usually positive; so this sadness that kept on bubbling up in me resulted in bits of anger towards myself. To aid with my overwhelming emotions, I kept writing and that gave me a healthy way to release my feelings. I wondered if LK knew I was angry and if she did, that would make me more angry. I realized in order to keep going, I had to abide in God's words and nourish my relationship with Him. I still knew that He was beyond good and that I would see His great faithfulness. At times of deep sadness, one just has to go with what they still know. I didn't know why God didn't heal Lila Kate as we wanted, I didn't know why I was hurting so much, and I didn't really know how to handle these emotions. There was, and still is, a host of "IDKs." That's the invitation to life as I came to learn. But I could, and still can, fall back on the unchanging truths of God, which my heart did know.

As this journey progressed, our pastor turned me onto the book of Psalms. The book was and is a lifeline especially when my emotions get into a tangle. Within many Psalms, one sees David dealing with various emotions including anger. He presents his anger to God in prayer; one sees David always devoted to prayer. He repeatedly can be seen as the one not trying to connect the dots but repeatedly spending time with the One who already has the dots connected. Sometimes David's anger is directed towards God; where other times it's not. It's a comfort to me knowing I can share any emotion with the Creator, King of Kings, and The Most High God. He already knows, but still He invites me to share with Him! Even when I don't know exactly what to pray or how to put my emotions into words, He promises His Spirit (Romans 8). He's bigger than big, yet cares about every single little emotion that I feel. The same is true for my reader!

# Adventure #19 – His Goodness Doesn't Change!

September 17, 2015

*God is good even when I can't see His goodness. I need to keep telling myself that.*

Over the years, I've learned I have to talk to myself rather than listen to my emotions or situation. While one must take into account one's feelings and others' feelings, it's important to learn not to let those feelings be our ultimate guide! Instead let the truth of God's words be the guide and not the truth of the feelings! Let those feelings only guide you towards the One who has allowed you to feel those feelings, like David does throughout the Psalms.

I know my reader has heard it before: the mind can be the

biggest enemy! Indeed, we each get into high uncharted waters, and we all have to "put up with the ugly" in some fashion. But God is still good. Nothing will change His goodness. His goodness is permanent. His goodness has to do with everything that He accomplished upon the cross, and with His glorious resurrection.

Yes, when one is struggling, it might be really hard to see God's goodness. But it's through my struggling moments, I see so clearly how these words fleshed out. "Through suffering we come to know Him better. He breaks up our confidence in ourselves. We develop compassion for others. We understand how much better God is than all earthly gifts, how he alone has the power over death, and how he is faithful..." (from *Not God Enough,* by J.D. Greear)

During a visit with our pastor, he gave me a children's book to share with the kiddos. He told me to take it home and see what I thought about it. And so I did. I had my dad read it to me right when we got home; and because it was a children's book, I naturally sat on his lap! The book was entitled *The Moon is Always Round* by Jonathan Gibson, and I highly recommend it for any age, especially parents who have a child in Heaven! The author uses the moon as a comparison tool in relating to God's goodness even when one can't see His goodness completely. Like the moon, our eye doesn't always see that the moon is always round just as our eye doesn't always see that God is good, but both are continually true statements. And for a good side note, I look at the moon more often these days!

# Adventure #20 – STORM

December 27, 2015

*Even as Peter was trusting God, doubt and fear tried to literally sink him.*

The popular story of Peter walking upon the water can be a shot of encouragement; especially on days when it feels like I'm sinking. At the time, we were coming up on the one year mark of LK's Heavenly homecoming, and the memories of the past Christmas break were a cheerful tune to the now sorrowful tune. For LK's last Christmas on Earth, Santa's sled delivered twin dolls with a tiny stroller that she thought was for her; and not the dolls. This playdate was a little longer than usual due to school being out and she was not allowing me to pause playing for a snack. Yes, now I know why I didn't pause for long for a snack (thanks, God); this would be our last earthy play date and felt food would have to do the trick. Yes, I've already shared this memory before but it's staying because it can!

During this specific season, I was still in close contact with The Puckett family. This family will always be some of my favorite people, as well as their extended family.. Specifically, I can note that God placed Jason and Cathy on my radar to show me how to keep going years after a little heart (or two) has been torn away from your physical grip. I included a text message that Cathy sent me a few years back which served as her answer to "How do you keep going?" In fact, both Cathy and Jason have always been there to encourage me with timely text messages throughout specific seasons. Through it all, I can smile when I reflect on all the weddings, golf outings, photo opps, cookouts and plain ole fun that I've shared with these friends!

As I'm writing, I recently read through the story of Peter again, and the lesson was absolutely perfect timing. I shared this in Adventure #42. God always amazes me when He takes a familiar Bible story and showers His goodness upon it, so it is exactly what my heart needs at the moment. Anyway, Peter was being obedient when he and his buddies were caught in a storm. Fear was very evident in each of their hearts, but the fear took on a new level when they saw "a ghost" walking on the water! Yet Peter decided to ask a big question and his faith was shown when he stepped out of the boat, realizing the person was Jesus! Yet when Peter fixed his attention on the storm, he started to sink. Still, Jesus reached out and saved Peter. This shows me perspective is almost everything and reminds me of the saying "Sometimes God calms the child (Matthew 14) or sometimes he calms the storm (Mark 4)."

As Cathy Puckett texted me in September of 2019:

*It takes faith daily. Faith in knowing that they are with God. Faith in knowing they are in no pain. Faith in knowing they will be waiting for me with open arms when it's my time to go home...It's okay to cry and it's okay to not be okay at times, but you have to ask God for strength to make it through each and every day. I can't even imagine the hurt God felt watching His only son die for our sins. You have to know that God's love is everlasting. Just because I can't physically touch my boys or see them... I often close my eyes and ask God to let me know they are okay...and He does just that. We can't stop living because we've suffered the ultimate loss...that should propel us into living the utmost for God's kingdom.*

*Just know you are not alone in your suffering, but you have to learn to just breathe and thank God for loving LK so much. He loves you just the same. You keep going sweet girl...God has plans for your life and you keep the faith. God's comfort and love never fails us.*

*I love you sweet girl and keep going!!!*

# Adventure #21 – God Gives and God Takes (By Skip McAlister)

January 1, 2016

*I wish Lila was here with me. But God gives and God takes. After all, Lila did belong to God first. One reason God gives is so we can give to others and maybe God takes away so we can give to others, too.*

As many of you know, Misty and I (Skip) lost our 3rd and youngest child on January 9, 2015. Our Lila Kate was born March 31, 2010, with Down's Syndrome, pulmonary hypertension, and a heart defect which required open heart surgery when she was just a few months old. Lila's first two and a half years were spent never getting out of the house much. She required oxygen 24 hours a day so we were very careful in not exposing her to a lot of people in fear of her getting whatever sickness was going around. It wasn't long after she was two and a half that doctors told us Lila only needed to have additional oxygen during the night. This was such great news because this meant we were now able to function more like a family. All of a sudden Lila was going everywhere!

Lila was the happiest and most loving child I have ever been around. She never greeted anyone without giving her famous hug and pat on the back. As one young man said, "Lila has taught me more about love than any man on earth." She was the best example of Christ-like love that I have ever been around. It was this kind of love that was the motivation for starting a memorial fund in her honor.

Within a week after Lila's funeral, Misty and a friend started kicking around the idea of having a 5K race to raise money for organizations that helped special needs children. This was when the *I Love Lila Kate Memorial Fund* was established. We formed a board of directors and went to work on raising money for a 5K race that was to be held on March 21, 2015. This specific date was very important to us because down syndrome is genetically referred to as trisomy 21. This specific date was very important to us because Down's Syndrome is genetically referred to as Trisomy 21. This is when there is an extra copy of chromosome 21. With God's help we were able to pull off the very first *I Love LK 5K* in just seven weeks. We had about 200 participants and raised $18,000, which we gave to local organizations focused on special needs children. God has continued to bless the *I Love LK Memorial Fund* and race. At last year's race there were over 600 runners/walkers signed up and we gave away $42,000! In all, the LK Memorial Fund has raised and given $150,000 to some wonderful local organizations in honor of our precious little girl. We are so thankful to God for putting this idea of a memorial fund in Misty's thoughts five years ago.

Not only has the LK Fund and race helped a lot of special

needs children, it has helped tremendously with the grieving our family has experienced with losing Lila Kate. Every time we see someone wearing a LK hat, or an LK 5K race t-shirt we just smile! We love hearing the stories of how people on vacation hundreds of miles away ran into someone wearing a LK shirt, or hat. It's truly amazing to see what God is doing through a little special needs girl who He called home after four and half years.

# Adventure #22 – I Can

November 1, 2016

*I can be all that God created me to be. I can be a light in this dark world. I can show others how God loves them. I can dance! This past weekend we had an opportunity to share the LK story at an "I Can of Arkansas" dance show. This was a first for us, a first for me being a guest speaker. Lila's love and passion for this life committed me to go forth and share her legacy of love.*

This particular semester at National Park Community College, I was the lucky duck enrolled in a communication class. I don't know who desires to give presentations, but there are a select few and I applaud them for it. But I was checking off that graduation checklist, so I enrolled. The catch was I enrolled to take this class on-line; I know, right? There were two speeches to be given during the semester, one persuasive speech and one informative speech, with a given audience of ten people or more. I don't recall my persuasive speech nor where I did it but my informative speech will be a special memory for me and it helped me knock out a passing grade, as well.

A local nonprofit organization called "I Can of Arkansas" invited the McAlister family to come share Lila's legacy and to inform others about their own nonprofit organization. Of course, the McAlister's were all in and agreed to share. But unfortunately, prior commitments prevented them from going, so I was asked if I would share. My first thought was no, but then on second thought I could kill two birds with one stone by knocking out an assignment and serving as a spokesperson for an organization which is dear to my heart. So I went, and I'm glad I did.

I honestly don't know how I gave a twenty-minute presentation. I was weak, but that's when God tends to strike a pose! I think He loves when His children step out in faith as He shows what He can do through them to hopefully be a blessing to someone else! Giving a presentation was the last thing I wanted to be doing, because what I really wanted to be doing was dancing up there on stage with LK, with me as her buddy. But God had different plans and that has to be okay.

Recently I was writing (surprising, right?!) and I thought God glued together some pretty cool words with the verb phrase, "I can." "Like many gifts, one must receive the gift as it's similar to God's gift of Jesus. Why would one not open a gift someone gave? For it was purchased with the very soul in mind, since the beginning and even before the beginning. And because of that single reason, I can step. I can step because God had me in mind since the beginning and even before the beginning. I can step because He knew the cost to restore my broken relationship with Him, but still He stepped down. I can step because I know that He is continually working through my pain to draw me closer to Him and maybe even others, too. I can step and so can you."

## This Little Light of Mine, November 2016

*If this world was all there was then I would give myself permission to basically do nothing and to not care. But this world isn't all there is. For the child of God, there is much more to come and much better to come!! I'm simply a traveler in this world; Heaven is my home!*

*I have cherished memories of our family going on a road trip and near the end of the trip everyone is past ready to get to the usually beautiful destination. When we get to our destination everyone usually agrees that the long road trip was worthwhile!! And how much more so for the child of God when we each reach our final destination of Heaven! I think we will say it's worthwhile.*

*One year when the McAlisters were on their own road trip, LK's diaper exploded. Ruh-roh! They pulled over to change the diaper only to find that the baby wipe container was almost empty. Double ruh-roh! Using all the wipes they had got her only semi clean. She wasn't a happy traveler, nor was anyone else at this point. This required her mom to climb in the back seat and start singing in weird voices. The song Mrs. McAlister picked, "This Little Light of Mine," singing it in funny voices to attempt to make Lila Kate laugh. The famous lyric "ain't no devil gonna blow it out," worked as a creative strategy to shift the focus off the dirty diaper! The dirty diaper was still very evident, and was eventually changed, but for that critical moment, the singing skills came in handy.*

*As I reflect on this priceless memory, God reminds me of His truth in Romans 8, where Paul encourages me to shift my perspective off these "dirty diapers" and compare them with the grandness of the eternal glory that God promises to those who turn to Him in faith. It's not denying the fact that we have a "dirty diaper" but it's viewing that "dirty diaper" with a perspective that it'll be changed one day. So while we can, let's shine our light even in a "dirty diaper" and not allow the devil to blow it out!*

# Adventure #23 – LK's 7th Birthday

March 31, 2017

*Pour LK's love into hungry little souls. Yes, it's exhausting on every level but everyone needs love. Love is the main ingredient.*

When Lila departed, I quickly noticed that it was a challenging task for me to be around little bodies. Anyone who knows me knows that I have a big heart for children, so this wasn't an ideal situation to be in. Even baby showers or the talk of other parents expecting a child (especially a girl) triggered a heaviness that stirred my questions and harsh emotions. It was the perfect picture of someone else receiving what God had taken away from other parents. Yes, this thought was selfish and I was falling into envy that I didn't want to fall into, but it's my sinful nature. Even now this may still happen to me, and it's something I must guard against. It doesn't always knock me completely out emotionally; however, when I fall into these little sinful traps, I'm reminded of Romans 7:18-25. Here Paul describes how he does the very action he hates, even though he desires to do right but can't because his heart is full of hate (sin). Yet, he closes with a picture of God's grace that is available to meet him (and us) where we are! Where would we be without the gospel? That question should encourage our hearts to share it all the more!

Anyway, as expected, LK's birthdays were super difficult without the main guest, especially the days leading up to it. The anticipation can be the most difficult for birthdays or "Heavenly homecomings." On Lila's birthday, the McAlisters always try to do something special with family and close friends. This particular year, LK's 7th birthday was on a Friday (which was a double emotional slam for me because Friday was our famous date night) and the McAlisters had a ballgame. In my mind, I should've been babysitting LK as they went to the game. As it turned out, I was babysitting but it wasn't for the child of my choice. The McAlisters asked me to hang out with the foster child who was staying with them at the time, so obviously I agreed because the joy usually outweighs the sadness. I clearly remember a text from Skip that particular morning while I was trying to get out of bed and the words can still be an encouragement to my heart:

*"Come play with and love on this baby girl the way you played with and loved on Lila...because love is worth it!"*

Yes! Love is worth it. Even nowadays, when loving on little hearts might trigger sadness, there is also so much joy. My LK memories always surface during playdates with small hearts; but most of the time it's like getting to share part of my LK time with someone else who desperately needs love. I say desperately because more times than not in this current season in my life, I get the opportunity to love on a bunch of different children who are in foster care (I'll share more specifically about the nonprofit organization that connects me with these children in part III). These are the ones who usually need the most love.

# Adventure #24 – allowing myself to be weak

June 20, 2017

*There are moments where floods of weakness will overflow one soul. In those moments, God is still there. In those moments, His grace is all the more profound.*

I find loads of encouragement from Paul's thorn in the flesh and it's interesting to me that a lot of theologians agree that Paul's thorn wasn't an actual thorn; some studies think it was something to do with eyesight or something else. But nonetheless, he pleaded with God multiple times to remove such pain! Instead God responded in a manner that Paul may have not been so fond of; God didn't remove the pain! (2 Corinthians 12). Why? Didn't God want Paul to live a pain free life? If you try to find a verse that proves such, you'll be searching for a longer than long time! God wasn't interested in making Paul's life a Candyland™ game, but instead God was fully interested in making Paul more like Him. And surprise, that's the same aspect that God is interested in for all His children! This isn't the first time (nor the last) I talk about Paul in this book, for he's noted in chapter eleven and chapter thirteen. Paul is indeed a "special tool" and one who experienced "hurting and hurting some more," too. Levi Lusko reflects on Paul's calling in Acts 9, with these words: "There are two elements there that we must not miss: (1) Paul would be used powerfully, and (2) Paul would suffer greatly. But I believe those are actually two sides of the same coin that exist within every calling." God didn't brush Paul's pain off as if it didn't matter but God wasn't going to remove a "temporary weakness" that could clearly show His "eternal power."

## Adventure #25 – Grief and Depression

September 25, 2017

*I want grief and depression to take a vacation.*

Unfortunately, grief and Depression are commonly linked together. But I wasn't too quick on claiming "I was depressed." To me, that was a dark word, with a wide range of definitions. In some cases, medical attention is required because it can be a chemical imbalance. Thankfully, God has provided doctors for such cases, but sometimes medical attention is not needed.

In my specific case, I don't think I ever suffered from Clinical Depression because in this case it's more continual and longer lasting. I think I tend to struggle more with Seasonal Depression, but it's not the "winter blues" it's the "summer blues." I might have a flare up I out of the ordinary but it's usually during the spring/summer when I struggle the most. I can look back at later entries and see the same types of struggles were faced two years in a row around April/May and running into August/September.

Sometimes I do consider seeing a doctor for an anti-depressant, but so far I've learned to manage it okay without. My biggest help through these periods is talking through it! That makes almost a world of a difference for me, for the better! As reaching out to someone is considered one of my positive outlets. I've also found healthier outlets to help me through such experiences, which I'll share below. As one may have gathered, time doesn't heal all wounds, but with time, God does heal. He heals little by little; until the day I'll be completely healed in Heaven! But until then, time does play an important role and gives one the chance to learn. Below I will share a brief overview of my personal struggles with Depression and what I try to do to manage it.

When I'm experiencing a "funky monkey," my biggest hurdles are extreme fatigue and an awkward heaviness in my heart that I wake up with and usually go to bed with. The heaviness can feel like trying to pick up a barbell that's simply too heavy! Grief is a barbell in itself but then the added weight of Depression creates a bigger workload. My fatigue is something that tends to happen when I'm trying to process too many emotions at once and sometimes I have trouble sorting out my emotions. That's why I have my healthy outlets so I can work through my emotions. My positive outlets usually include writing, reading, reaching out to someone to talk to, as well as being sure I'm getting plenty of physical activity, along with healthy calories. During a depressive spell I can literally wake up exhausted, even after an adequate amount of sleep, and simply not feel like going forward with the day. Yes, that was a shock for me at first because I'm usually a morning person. But the days truly felt like they should be over before I even touched my feet to the floor. I experienced physical depletion on every level. When I am going through one of these episodes, my mornings and my nights tend to be the worst because those are the slower parts of my day.

These days I have a better acceptance of what happened, but I still might wonder "why" I'm experiencing these types of struggles. Yes, I've learned how to be easier with myself (and others). I can accept my hard emotions most of the time without always getting upset at myself for feeling whatever I'm feeling. This single strategy has done wonders for me. This definitely took patience, and I still have to remember to be careful with my emotions from time to time. I've learned how to manage my "funky monkeys" so much better now with the positive outlets I shared above. Such heavy times are more spread apart than they were before, but God still uses them to teach me how to depend more on Him and others, and less on myself. I've seen God's faithfulness time after time. He continues to provide what I need at just the right moment whether it's a "spot on verse" from my bible reading, a timely devotional, encouragement from a friend, or a visit with our pastor or someone else that I feel comfortable talking to.

## LK's prayer, September 2017

*"Dear God, I pray. Amen." That's the little prayer Lila learned which thrilled everyone. It wasn't typical of her to put this many words together, so this was literally like a mouthful. She usually communicated with actions and indeed had a lot to say without using words! She would giggle at funny moments and cry in sad or frustrating moments. Yes, she knew how to answer yes and no questions, for her favorite word was "no." The typical child! Lila knew names and spoke a handful of them, but to have a full vocal conversation with her was not common. Her siblings taught her a handful of little phrases and to see their hearts in action with their sister was the kind of sight every parent wants to see. All siblings have their moments, but both of them still helped take care of their younger sissy.*

*For this simple little prayer, she would fold her hands and close her eyes while repeating what mamma or daddy said. My memories are foggy but I do remember the "Dear God, I pray. Amen." And how amazing for this disabled child to put together a sentence AND direct it to the Creator? That's lovely stuff right there. I need to forever hang on to that memory, for it reminds me that God hears the smallest cries of our hearts.*

# Adventure #26 – Gloomy Days

October 24, 2017

*A dark cloud hangs over me, yet God has been so good to me. I know He is always good and always loves me even on days like today.*

Our days upon Earth can be dark, cold, and gloomy. It's the cold of winter, but yesterday felt like Spring. Death is only a stepping stone for the child of God into the everlasting beauty and light of Him. On that day, our faith will become sight!! One of the famous lines which our pastor continually shared with me throughout this dark season was "God still loves on gloomy days." The popular story of Noah and the ark flashes in my thoughts when I ponder gloomy days. Noah is known for walking with God (Genesis 6:9) along with one of my favorites, Enoch! In the Bible all that is recorded about Enoch is that he walked with God! There's not a better attribute to be remembered for. Enoch didn't even face physical death, for when God was ready for him to come home, he simply disappeared. At least that's what I gather from the text in Genesis 5:24. The action of walking with God doesn't mean you're perfect. In fact, it's likely the very opposite. I walk with God because I realize I'm not perfect and will never meet God's standards on my own. Even Noah made mistakes at the end of the flood (Genesis 9:21), and yet Noah still walked with God and was one that God used. Noah walked with God even when it was really dark, and obeyed God even when others disagreed with what he was doing. What came after Noah's gloomy days? Yes, the rainbow! What if the beautiful rainbow never came? Common sense tells me I probably wouldn't stick around, but I think Noah would've continued to obey God and look to Him for protection. May I learn to do the same.

Noah probably knew he was a traveler upon this earth and that he had His loving Father holding him. He also had others who were linked together with him who shared a like mind. Let's note how one can be like Noah: walking with God even on gloomy days, knowing we are a traveler upon earth, and linking ourselves together with like-minded friends. And just like God used Noah's dark clouds to show a glimpse of His light, maybe one day God will use your dark clouds to show another soul a glimpse of His light!

In my grief experience, the gloomy days can still pop out of nowhere and the silver linings seem to fade too fast. But in those moments I can remember what J. D. Greear says: "Sometimes we may not be able to see the silver lining behind the dark cloud. But the cross is evidence that it's there." That specific quote is special to me for not only is it a wonderful quote, but when it pops up, I automatically reflect on my friendship with one of the girls at church named Ashley who is an absolute blessing to probably all she meets. I know this reflection from her will be a special blessing to you, too:

*Rather long post for me, but worth sharing...*

*Allie and I have been working our way through a book called Not God Enough by J.D. Greear. The chapter I was reading through tonight used the analogy of our lives as tapestries. Here's what it said:*

"If all you could see were the backside of a tapestry as it was being woven, you would conclude that nothing beautiful was taking shape. When you flipped it to look at it from the front, however, you see that every strand finds its perfect place according to the plan of the artist. Not one thread in our lives is out of place. Jesus is never absent, never forgetful, and never late."

*I am guilty of getting frustrated when I don't understand "the plan" in my life or when things don't end up how I wanted or on my timeline. I've messed up over and over and when you feel like the mess you've made is beyond fixing and just chaos, He gives you a peak at the front of the tapestry that's being woven when you allow Him to be the artist.*

~ Ashley Loe, July 2019

## Adventure #27 – Children's Books

April 8, 2019

*The children's book aisle is by far not my favorite aisle at the store anymore.*

My favorite activity to do with Lila Kate was jumping into books together and usually more than once! I remember I tended to make up stories about the pictures just as she did when she read her version to me. I would imitate the given characters, showing excitement, disappointment, or some different emotion that I thought the character might be experiencing. On this particular day, it seemed as if all the characters were experiencing big sadness. Yet the characters were still playing an active part in the story, and that's what I'm continually learning to do, even to this day.

There are numerous little aspects that trigger my grief to flare up, but I've learned how to manage my emotions so much better and not every little aspect sends me for an emotional whirlwind. For example, today I was at another book aisle. But, instead of letting my bitter emotions take over, I tried to practice thankfulness. I literally stopped and thanked God for the books that LK and I shared. Or another example, sometimes, when others are talking about a new baby on the way or the conversations of what to get their toddler for a birthday or Christmas, and it just happens to be a princess castle (of course LK had one), I will try to pause and practice thankfulness. I simply want to run away and avoid the entire conversation, because even if it's just background noise, it can still create an ill effect in my heart. No wonder it's so easy to slip down into self-pity and isolate yourself from others, but that's not how God created me to live! I realize the person probably doesn't even know that's an emotional stab for me and it's not like God created me to be at the center of everything. A side note to share here is found in one of my favorite books titled *Not God Enough*, the author actually references Nicolaus Copernicus' findings which describe how the sun is actually at the center of the universe instead of the earth. The author writes;

"As it turns out, it's a good thing the earth isn't the center of our solar system because it simply does not have the gravitas to keep all the other planets in orbit. Our sun does, and so it keeps all the planets, including ours, safely and securely in orbit. Copernicus's revolution has an important corollary to our lives: Our lives don't work when we make ourselves the center of our own little universe either, even if God is one of our orbiting planets. We don't have the gravitas to keep it all together."

So there I have it, I'm not the center of my own little world! And because of that, I certainly don't want to steal their joy or their excitement. I've learned that these little stabs are all over, but what once made me sick to my stomach, now can be an opportunity to thank God for what He did give me. I can now be okay with feeling a little heart tug. These little tugs remind me that I'm not yet healed from what happened, and even when I'm simply going along enjoying life, those little tugs can still be there and that's okay, too. I have learned how to be okay with what's really not okay.

## Adventure #28 – Church Family

April 12, 2019

*Sometimes "church family" simply feels like an extension of family.*

I've been fortunate to not remember a time when I wasn't plugged into a church family. My family has been going to the same church since I was in 1st grade. My heart hurts for those who aren't actively plugged into a local church family, but the truth is, church can be hard. It's hard for a variety of reasons and maybe it's hard when I focus solely on myself instead of on God and others. In my opinion, there's a difference between simply going to church and being an active member within a local body of believers. I'll be straightforward and admit that the young hearts have been the ones keeping me getting up each Sunday morning and going to church. I shared about this previously as those small hearts were key instruments early in my grief journey, as well as now. Nonetheless, church is still hard! My current read is Life After the Death of my Son by Dennis L. Apple. While I don't relate to every aspect of his grief, God still uses these kinds of books to bring me comfort, as they show me that I'm not alone, even years after such a loss. Apple describes going to church perfectly by saying, "I love my church, but sometimes it hurts to be there." He nailed it, regardless of the grief stricken person!

Nonetheless during this particular season in my life, I found some new opportunities of how to build a few new friendships within our church family. I was continually looking for a ride after class and many times one of the ladies from church would graciously come pick me up and a simple car ride would become the highlight of my days. During those rides, I was able to better know the person and hopefully they got to know me a bit more. I found the ladies lunch group and shared lunch with them often. We started a book together, and I was able to get to know some of them while nourishing a friendship with God, too. Once in a while, I went on visits to our "shut ins" (to see those who lived in nursing homes or others who can't get out very often) and those were my favorite. Most of the time, people simply wanted someone to talk to. It helped me by simply talking or laughing, especially on days when I was experiencing hard emotions, because these people were too.

I'm resistant to sharing names because there has been a mighty army within my church family, and even outside our local church family, of people who have been there to help me out when I needed help. Whether it was giving me a car ride or simply their presence. I often forget what people say, but I usually don't forget who has been there. Time and time again that's what makes the biggest difference, being there. I do have some names to share though because these are specific people who indeed have been used to help shape me!

As shared previously, Ashley and I went through the Not God Enough book together and it was such a blessing to me in a unique way. She would come visit me after work weekly as we talked about the previous chapter in our book. We would simply share some small talk, which did my soul good. Fast forward to present, this entire family has been key in my moving forward in my grief. They have two small girls, who remind me of what Lila and I might be doing these days. While at times it's still soul crushing, it's also soul healing, too. God still uses the smallest tools to help me continue forward.

Kay is one of the ladies who was my favorite ride to almost anywhere! She would spoil me (yes, I'll admit it), and we would always share good conversations about the Bible or something meaningful. She's very passionate about God's word and everyone needs a "Kay" in their lives! When always found a store to stop in or a project at church to work on, like planting flowers or painting the cabinets in our Sunday School classroom.

Cody is probably a blessing to everyone he meets! He was a blessing in disguise for me and our family. I have shared some about him previously in the book. He was actually the first person that I felt comfortable sharing Lila Kate with from an emotional standpoint, other than our pastor. The way God crossed our paths will always remind me that God tends to answer prayers in ways that are bigger and much cooler than what we originally asked. I love Cody and love (tolerate) our friendship! I'll forever be thankful for him and the visits over meals that he has shared with our family!

In her book, *Church is Hard*, Brianna Freelen says this:

"Church is hard for the person walking through the doors, afraid of judgment. Church is hard for the pastor's family, under the microscope of an entire body. Church is hard for the prodigal soul returning home, broken and battered by the world. Church is hard for the girl who looks like she has it all together, but doesn't. Church is hard for the couple who fought the entire ride to service. Church is hard for the single mom, surrounded by couples holding hands and seemingly perfect families. Church is hard for the widow and widower with no invitation to lunch after service. Church is hard for the deacon with an estranged child. Church is hard for the choir member overwhelmed by the weight of the lyrics in that song. Church is hard for the man insecure in his role as a leader. Church is hard for the wife who longs to be led by a righteous man. Church is hard for the nursery volunteer who desperately longs for a baby to love. Church is hard for the single woman and single man, praying God brings them a mate. Church is hard for the teenage girl, wearing a scarlet letter, ashamed of her mistakes. Church is hard for gays, adulterers, liars, cheats, and slanderers. Church is hard for the sinners. Church is hard for me. It's hard because on the outside it all looks shiny and perfect. Sunday best in behavior and dress. However, underneath those layers, you find a body of imperfect people, carnal souls, selfish motives. But, here is the beauty of church—Church isn't a building, mentality, or expectation. Church is a body. Church is a group of sinners, saved by grace, living in fellowship as saints. Church is a body of believers bound as brothers and sisters by an eternal love. Church is a holy ground where sinners stand as equals before the Throne of Grace. Church is a refuge for broken hearts and a training ground for mighty warriors. Church is a converging of confrontation and invitation. Where sin is confronted and hearts are invited to seek restoration. Church is a lesson in faith and trust. Church is a bearer of burdens and a giver of hope. Church is a family. A family coming together, setting aside differences, forgetting past mistakes, rejoicing in the smallest of victories. Church, the body, and the circle of sinners-turned-saints, is where He resides, and if we ask, He is faithful to come."

## Adventure #29 – children's books

June 14, 2019

*Someone shared their testimony at church tonight, and God used this to encourage me to keep going. My every spare moment has been hurting.*

As I key the letters, it's September 2021. I'm currently finishing my first edit through part two of this book. It's another one of those "soul crushing and soul healing" moments for me. It seems as if every time I reach a healthy target in the whole book project, my emotions crash. No, it's not a famous "funky monkey," but it's definitely a tickle in my throat. A few months ago, I came across a video of Misty talking with LK, who was probably about four months old. In the video, Misty was telling LK that "one day you will get off this oxygen and go meet everyone," and all the while LK is already talking all about it! That video is still almost soul crushing to watch, but it is also soul healing! God has used that video to encourage my heart, especially with the process of writing this book. Because there were numerous times when I wanted to just be done already or not go forth, but the truth is, I need this book. I need this book so I can keep going, because through it, I've clearly seen that God doesn't waste pain! He doesn't always make the pain disappear, but He does use it, as I'll share again in the next entry, because it's worth repeating to myself right now.

Untimely we each have a story. Our stories can be used by God to encourage others, comfort others, and simply show others more of God. I'm not sure how He does it, but it's a pretty amazing thing to watch Him go about it. Keep in mind that you and I aren't the main characters in our story. Our story isn't necessarily ours. I realize that sounds odd, but really we are each simply little tools in God's big hands! It's His story that we are privileged to be a part of by His amazing grace. It's His story that is greater, and that is worth repeating by our words and our actions.

## Adventure #30 – life

November 2, 2019

*It's full of twists and turns, ups and downs, but it's always moving forward. Accept the gift.*

God's faithfulness is actually indeed higher than the clouds, all the little random happenings aren't random at all, and God will shine His goodness even at the darkest of night because He is beyond good. That's what I've been gathering as I jumped into the process of writing this book. And that's simply what I want to leave my reader with. This is just a beautiful, crazy ride called life. As I stated upon the start of this book, for years I've been the type to record a short journal entry of basically silly day events, any worries that are kind of heavy, and Bible study notes. As I used my notebooks to aid in writing this book, I've taken many trips down memory lane exploring those old roads, and oh my goodness, it's so rewarding and challenging to see how all the hills and valleys, all the twists and turns, and all the hurt and joy intersect with each other. It seems that one almost can't have one without the other.

As I shared earlier, writing has always been something I've enjoyed, but it wasn't until after LK experienced her "Heavenly homecoming" that God showed me how writing could be used as an outlet for my craze of hard emotions as well as a testament of my seemly wavering mustard seed faith. Regardless, I found writing to be a gift from Him, one He wants me to use to bring honor and glory to His Name! We can never bring enough praise to Our Savior; He rescued us from sin's grip, gave us life in His holy name, and so much more! He's my "good, good father," as the song says, and as I know.

And because of that, there IS purpose in the pain. There is. By no means does the ache disappear, but it can definitely be used in His hand and through His ways. Simply ponder the cross where Christ said, "Into your hands, I commit my spirit." (Luke 23:46). Before He died, we can see the pain literally running down in red drops as well as the drops of sweat that poured from his face. All for the purpose of seeing our face, and us seeing Him fully in all boldness. Not just in Heaven one day, but here, too. Here we can see His reflection through His word. Here we can boldly approach his throne to find grace and mercy (Hebrews 4:16), and I believe there's so much more that He wants to show us!

# Part 3:
# My Life Now, and How I Still Struggle Sometimes

Twenty-One Adventures & More

## Adventure #31 – February 18, 2021

I'm anxiously waiting to take the next steps in actually seeing a book come together here! The waiting is extremely difficult. Surprisingly, the waiting is harder than writing the actual book. Though I'm thankful for God making all the right connections along the way and again all in coincidences! Yes, I'm fully aware that there are no such things as coincidences, that it's actually God's hand going before me and directing my path. Really I see my big picture idea still being played out by God crossing my paths with the right person at the right time, specifically in the writing/publishing process. Nonetheless waiting is still a hard part, but Part 3 was completed during a waiting period as well as a few flashbacks to 2020 writings. I was already in the healthy habit of writing daily, and now I see that part 3 was really needed for the book. I was waiting and reaching out to different people who could edit my book, make my cover come to life, and simply make my book come to life. At first, I wanted God to connect me with someone I knew to edit the book because it was a tough project to complete and then proceed to share. Yes, I know God will allow eyes to read this that I may not meet until Heaven, but for me to sit down and work through such a project, I felt like the person would need to be someone I knew and could be open with.

Anyway, the book is all I can really think about. Did I write all God wanted me to? Do the words flow? Do I live out my words? Am I doing the right thing? All kinds of thoughts. And then as I write, the wonderful, beautiful, and amazing snowfall that we've recently experienced triggers some sadness. I love watching the snowflakes fall and remembering that it's a life-giving picture of being covered in God's righteousness when He made my sins as white as snow, but other thoughts wiggle into my mind: Would LK adore the snow? Why didn't we get a snow picture? Does it snow in Heaven? As these thoughts tumble forward, I have to repeat to myself that I'm okay.

I'm okay because I know who is holding on to my heart and I'm trying to hang onto His, too. It has been said and I totally feel these words that I came across not too long ago; "Grief on a normal day is a dull ache that you learn to endure. On an abnormal day, grief is a heart wrenching pain that refuses to be ignored. If you're having one of those days, close your eyes and picture yourself crawling up in your Father's lap, laying your tear-stained face against His strong shoulder, and baring your broken heart. Imagine His arms enfolding you and holding you firmly while you feel your life as you had imagined it would be shattered into a million pieces. Hold tightly onto Him; but if you can't, that's okay, because He's holding tightly onto you."

This morning my reading met me where I was and I was actually praying yesterday that I just needed one more "something" to confirm I'm doing the right task with this writing project. Then this morning, Gideon visited me. I love Gideon! He also needed a lot of confirmation that he was on the right track doing what God wanted him to (Judges 6). Of course, God wanted to use Gideon to save the Israelites, but Gideon felt too inadequate so he asked for a sign (multiple times) from God to confirm His direction. Guess what? God confirmed not once, but twice! It was just as Gideon requested, and for me this was a timely reminder!

The following is a little piece from one of my many notebooks:

February 22, 2020

*So here I am, we are at a new notebook to fill with the maybe unexpected things along the way. Sure, I pray God teaches me unexpected things that I'll note down for a reading reflection. But too, I know the unexpected can be scary, too. The events of January 9, 2015 were unexpected, but somehow God teaches me through the unexpected to expect to find HIM in everything—even the ugly unexpected events. So I'll keep going even when I don't want to. God has placed people around me, and we can continue to keep going one step at a time. All the while keeping focus on Jesus—or trying to—I fail daily especially in this area!*

*It's the plain ole truth that I think of Lila Kate daily. Every ounce of me misses every ounce of her. I would still go back, but I want to go forward, too. Yes, it's complicated at times. But I want to go forward; that's the only way for me to continue to see how God uses this pain for His glory. To go forward doesn't mean forgetting about Lila Kate and I don't think it means not hurting anymore. But instead it simply means allowing God to continue to work. To be open to what He has. So here I am, let's be open to what God has in store. I can be open to His work because I belong to Him and I know who He says I am. And, I know. He's my "good, good father" … as the song says, and as I know.*

## Adventure #32 – February 19, 2021

As I'm waiting to take my next steps with my first self-published book, I decided it'll help me to do a daily entry. It's a healthy exercise for me and doing so will hopefully sharpen my writing skills and capture various aspects. As I noted in one of my previous entries, the waiting is especially difficult. But even as I jump back to reflect on the first step of working on my book, I stated that I wish I could simply see the cover as I remind myself that writing a book is indeed a process. A process in which there are new waters for me. A process which involves (in my case) jumping back and forth across the timeline. And there's the word again: time. God has the perfect timing. As I'm waiting; He's working. I remind myself again. He's working all the time but sometimes it's easy to mistake our "waiting periods" for His "not working" periods … which is far from the truth. God is constantly working and maybe He does some of His greatest works through not only pain, but through waiting.

Even God has a process of doing such. One can see the concept of God's processes from the beginning of the world. I heard the following comparison somewhere and I reflect on it often: God took six full days to create this beautiful world, which man has ruined with sin. Who's to say God couldn't have created the world in a matter of a single day, or a single moment? He's God, after all! He's fully capable of anything. There was nothing in His way, but instead He decided upon a process. Why? I don't know. He's God! Maybe He wanted to teach us that even He has a unique process of doing such. And the creation story isn't the last time we see the concept of God's unique process. A handful of instances fly across my mind including Jesus' first miracle, the Israelites marching around the walls, and plenty more, but those two instances remind me to obey even when it seems so strange.

So in that regard, I'm trying not to rush things along, I have seen God's faithfulness time and time again. Plus, this life disappears fast enough. Doesn't it? A mist. A vapor. Gone. And yet, this life still matters. It's in this life that one makes the decision about Jesus or not. That's the life changing and life giving decision one must make in this life. Once one has felt the Holy Spirit's tug, it's simply the beginning. Day by day I attempt to yield to Him and allow Him to do His creative work in me, for He's only capable of making beautiful pieces. And somehow all the pieces fit, each in their own little way. I can't force a piece where it doesn't belong and I can't see how every piece fits, but in the same way that I trust the image on a cardboard puzzle box made by sinful hands, surely I can trust the sinless hands which took the nails for me and the rest of mankind.

With most puzzles, such a task is better tackled together. Also, puzzles require a great deal of patience. Both of these instances are comparable to our crazy ride of life. After the puzzle is completed, it's rewarding to see the beautiful picture and how even the seemingly odd pieces did indeed fit. As it will be in Heaven one day, but for now Paul reminds us that we simply see in part (1 Corinthians 13) and I'm reminded that we all need each other and that means we all need patience, too. I realize I have more than enough reasons to trust the grand "puzzle designer," who has given me glimpses of His beautiful puzzle time and time again!

# Adventure #33 – February 26, 2021

I'm hurting too much this morning. It's cold and dreary outside, comparable to my heart. Plus, this kind of weather can easily mess with my emotions. Yesterday while finding a Easter dress for a little girl in foster care in all my beautiful and painful memories surfaced. I've shared this before and may do so again because I'm allowed to do so! Lila's yellow dress. Third birthday. Successful cardiologist appointment. All triggers for my emotions to spin. Lila's 3rd birthday was on Easter Sunday and days before she received an outstanding report from the cardiologist. Everyone was excited and maybe a bit apprehensive about ditching the oxygen during the daytime. But luckily the transition was smooth, which resulted in mommy and daddy showing their little girl off, just as the doctors ordered.

A year and a half later, the dark clouds appeared and this

time the clouds were too much. Too weighty. Too dark. The clouds cried as Heaven rejoiced. It sucked. It still sucks today, given my human perspective. Yet, there's hope. Jesus. What came after the ugliness upon the cross? The ugliness was needed to create beauty for mankind. The ugliness still remains but the beautiful remains, too. And one day, we shall see the beautiful in full color.

As I punch the keys on the keyboard, my heart is warmed by God reminding me of some of His truths. Not only the ugliness of grief shed by Jesus which resulted in the beautiful joy of being reunited with man (Hebrews 12:2), but this morning in my quiet time, I read about the calling I have in Christ. Christ calls each of us to look beyond our human perspective to the "things that are unseen" because it is those things that will last (2 Corinthians 4:18). One of my favorite verses follows the same concept, says "For now we see in a mirror dimly, but then face to face. Now I know in part; then I shall know fully, even as I have been fully known." (1 Corinthians 13:12) This verse keeps popping up in various ways so I suppose God is trying to remind me of this truth!

## Adventure #34 – March 14, 2021

Birthday preparations are usually favored by most. Of course it depends on the age I suppose. Cheer. Happiness. Laughs. Cake. The recipe for birthday fun, except when the main guest is absent. Unfortunately, that's still the case this year for the one who I still consider my best friend. It's the hardest aspect of waking up every day, regardless of birthday month or not.

We've done this whole birthday thing in Heaven too many times that I know it's hard stuff, but this year the hard stuff has been magnified. She would be eleven years old so all my pictures probably don't match up with what she looks like now. I'm attached to the baby pictures and yes I'm thankful for such, but LK in an eleven-year old body is something I can't grasp. That thought alone crushes my heart so much. I'm not claiming we age in Heaven, but I do indeed spin my thoughts enough with this. It's mentally draining. It's not the birthday preparations I had in mind, and even after four birthdays with the little sassy pants in Heaven, it seems like it gets harder each year!

But God does the hard work with His children. He did the hardest work for His children on the cross and because of that single truth His children can do hard, too. LK memory: 3rd birthday came with a fabulous report from the cardiologist which allowed for decreased use of oxygen. This allowed the permission to show LK off to the watching world! The reality of that statement runs chills to my back because it's so true. I think God is actually the one who keeps showing LK off to a watching world as we continue to share LK's love and legacy even if it's much, much different and harder than we expected. God still does the hard, and even the harder, with us!

Here's what I wrote in one of my notebooks when I thought about Lila's birthday last year:

*10th birthday. I'll write but what should I write? There are so many words to grab from but yet still many more emotions to wrap my head around. For the moment I have stopped trying to grasp God's plan because time and time again He has shown me that His ways are higher than my ways and His thoughts are higher than my thoughts (Isaiah). My heart can rest in this truth and still ache. As we look at our world today, I think it's okay to be discouraged. In fact, I think the condition of the world hurt Jesus from the beginning, when the first people chose themselves over Him. Yet all throughout Scripture, we see an infinite, holy God shower compassion on His hurting people time and time again. When the Israelites were enslaved to the Egyptians, we see that God was moved to pity when He heard their cries for help. I love the repetition of the wording in Exodus 2, "God heard...God saw...God knew."*

*Not only that but He did something and a lot of somethings to reach the promised land. At one point He chose the weakest, smallest, and youngest of the clan to be Israel's first king, (1 Samuel) and in another instance He actually raised up one Israel's enemies to be an instrument to save His own people (Habakkuk). One of my favorites is this book of Habakkuk! The simple summary (of which I'll share again because it's one of my favorites) that our pastor shared with me goes like this: "I may not see what God is doing, I may not understand what God is doing. But I can always trust what God is doing." I may be jumping around in history and I get confused where these events fall, but the point is the same. Time after time we are placed in impossible situations where we are indeed the underdog, and time after time again we see God's plans unfold—even when the waters are rough, the fire is hot, and the mountain is big. Yes, It's so easy to be consumed with those rough waters, hot fires, and big mountains, but as we cling to Our Father and His promises we definitely see a glimpse of His perfect plan of redeeming mankind!!*

*As I write, I have my Pandora playing like usual and I noticed more songs about Heaven today. Maybe they play all the time but I still think it's a way of God comforting my heart today. Today is Lila Kate's 10th birthday. It seems so small compared to everything else that is going on with this pandemic and yes it is, but I find so much comfort in the fact that God is mindful of big and little aches alike. He never says "that's too little or that's too big." God is mindful of us and that's a truth that we can praise Him for even as we are hurting. He is so mindful that He went forth with the cross for me and for you! The latest song by Jeremy Camp has been on replay for the last several weeks and I'll share some lyrics because the song speaks volumes to my heart, "Whatever I face. Whatever the fear. Whatever the cost. You always draw near. Whatever the pain. Whatever may come. Whatever may fall. Your love overcomes."*

I want to close with some memories because it's harder to begin writing memories sometimes but thinking of a funny memory can make me laugh and bring me happiness. Like when we would read books and I talked in different funny voices just to make LK laugh, which would end up in both of us laughing together and probably forgetting the purpose for laughing in the first place! LOL. She loved swinging in the hammock and attempting to sing with the birds but when she sang the birds would disappear so I suppose it was now a "one man show." LOL. Lila loved music and music had no choice to love her back! She could tell us when "Luke" was on the radio (meaning Luke Bryan) and she and her sister would put on the wobble dance and many other dance moves. On the "ROAR" song by Katy Perry, LK learned how to literally yell the word roar on queue as it came along in the lyrics. LOL. This is the child who was completely okay with taking more than one bubble bath on Saturdays, who had french fries as an all-time favorite food, and who still just happens to be my best friend!!

Even though this journey has random highs and lows; all of life does. But I can say the lows are more spread apart and don't seem to last as long. I'm thankful for the unexpected beautiful doors that God has opened for me to share this journey with others and I'm sure He'll open more as I continue to step.

## Adventure #35 – March 20, 2021

As I write Spring Break Trip 2021 is under way! I'm hoping it will do me good because lately I've hit another funky monkey. This past month has been sticky. The birthday anticipation has literally tried to kill me while this book anticipation has me eager to see what God might continue to do through my pain. I know, it's quite the healthy balance. It is healthy to desire Heaven, but my longing for Heaven has been a bit too much lately. This is actually very normal when it comes to grieving a child who ran to heaven and needs to be addressed accordingly. So the first time this happened, it was extremely hard to share as I noted before. But thankfully, this time around wasn't as tough to share. I shared with trusted friends and now I'm off to the beach. I need to enjoy this trip so that's why I'm writing before as a way to hopefully release all this mixture of emotions.

God seems to be taking me the long way to the other side of this grief and it reminded me of the Israelites traveling. The Israelites were God's people in the Bible and even God led the Israelites on the long way to the promised land (Exodus 13). While it was due to their own sinful actions that resulted in the long way, we too are on the long way to Heaven due to us each being born with a sinful nature. If we each didn't have a sinful nature, we wouldn't know the hurt of being away from Christ nor others who have gone to Heaven before. Yet, Christ came and that's where everything changes.

Anyway, God has again met me right where I've been struggling and it involves the simple encouragement from two friends! Never underestimate the power of one's words; the tongue can indeed start a wildfire as James states among the other vivid pictures included in his letter. The two lines that were shared with me and I keep reminding myself of were shared by Cade and Cody, "There's still work that God wants to accomplish through you and while Heaven is going to be beyond beautiful it's all in God's timing" and "We each go through hard stuff and it can be an opportunity for God to use us to help someone else." As I see, God made us for relationships and no person is an island. We need others to speak words of love and encouragement into our lives. While the greatest blessing can be a friend who simply shows up, a tiny word of encouragement can be a game changer.

## Adventure #36 – April 9, 2021

I'd like to pick back up with my daily entries, even though not all of them are shared in this book, but my favorites are included. God has given me another day to write and one day I won't get such upon this earth so might as well write today. I know, it's been a minute since my daily entries and that seems to happen to me a lot! I start and then I stop! A miracle in itself that I completed my first draft of this book—I think it took me six to seven months to complete. I'm bubbling with eagerness to move to the next step. I'm excited that I'm excited. At first my feelings weren't bubbling with excitement. Often tough emotions and questions crept in, because really this isn't necessarily the book that I wanted to write, but I do think God wanted me to write it! Yes, I'm thankful for the ability to write, to capture memories and all the coolness of what God has shown me through this process. And when I try to imagine what all God could continue to do through this book. The hearts He'll touch. The hearts that I may not know until Heaven. That's simply mind blowing to me. That's my motivation. The people that God may touch. Even if it's one then it's worth it to me. I think about the parable of the lost sheep and how we are called to love, serve, and share to change that one sheep's world. How thankful I am that Christ would be willing to still come even for one sheep. One person. I must remind myself of those amazing life-giving truths, because honestly such truths get me from one day to the next.

I've been a major funky monkey. And I'm so over it! It started with the dreadful anticipation of LK's 11th birthday, which is expected to be tough but this particular year was a toughness overload. I wanted Heaven too much and too quick. It's okay to want Heaven but not too quickly. As I noted in my last entry, I was reminded that there are still people God wants me to share with, to give to, and simply to love! The same is true for you. If you are still on this earth, God still wants to use you!

Regardless, I was overwhelmed with eagerness to see LK. To see if she's actually an eleven-year- old, wondering what she looks like, and if she does typical eleven-year-old activities? I'm not sure. But I am sure of God's grace, which a friend reminded me is more than enough. Here again is Paul visiting. My reader already knows I absolutely love the story of Paul with his thorn in the flesh. He pleads for the pain to disappear yet it doesn't. It doesn't, so that God's strength can be magnified through such weakness. Do I relate to Paul right here? Yes!

I was expecting to bubble back into my typical bubbly self after LK's birthday, but I haven't yet. And I don't quite know why. I am exhausted from being exhausted, if that makes sense. It barely makes sense to me. I don't try to make sense of God's bigger plan, but it would be helpful to make sense of these emotions. It's hard work and I easily get overwhelmed with my emotions or simply because at times I can't pinpoint what they are. It's hard to work through. I realize emotions are simply part of being human, but the reaction to them is where one must respond and not just react. There's a difference.

This time last year I wrote in my notebook *"....that it feels good to help other people. It's like if you were a flat bike tire, and helping others is the air pump that pumps you back up. Those are words of wisdom from a little girl at church when she was doing a task with her daddy yesterday and it literally made my heart smile!! Let's be honest we all get that flat tires some days and in some cases those tires can randomly go flat. Yes, we know to check the tires for low pressure and we do but still the tire can randomly go flat in some cases. So what do we do? Well I think one must be prepared for those flats, having the right tools, recalling past experiences, and in some cases reaching out for assistance from another rider.*

One of my hobbies is biking, and last year my dad and I put in plenty of miles with a group from church. We would have Saturday morning rides along the back roads, downtown area, and even West mountain, which was my favorite! I remember one instance where I was the one who got a flat tire. Being a beginner rider, I didn't have my handy tool bag, nor really any past experience to gather from. Thankfully another person in our group did, and he was able to give me air, allowing us to continue the ride.

So looking at life in general, those flat tires are going to happen. In John 16, before Jesus left his disciples, he told them plainly that they would have trouble. I'm sure this wasn't easy for them to hear. Think about it, he just told them he's leaving and well trouble will still be here. I'm sure that wasn't what they wanted to hear! Yet, he didn't leave the conversation hanging there. The whole conversation from John chapters fourteen through sixteen are some of my favorites. I think it's interesting that Jesus is preparing them for his departure by giving the command of abiding in Christ by His Spirit which he says is better than having Him in flesh. He comforts their hearts about going to prepare a place in His Father's house and doesn't want them to live in fear. He reminds the disciples not to fear multiple times within these few chapters, and promises that the sorrow will one day be turned into joy. So back to our analogy, as a child of God I can be equipped with the right tools, I can recall God's past faithfulness, and I can reach out for others' help when needed. I'm thankful to be able to do all three of those when I experience a flat tire. God is mindful of little things and big things alike! Nothing is too small for Him nor too big!

## Adventure #37 – April 14, 2021

I was considering the task of counseling, because this "funky monkey" has been longer than usual. I was on week six when it's usually not more than two weeks. I wanted someone who knew how special LK is and someone who knew the story. So I prayed on it and God brought a specific name to mind. I reached out with the following text message to Lamar Trieschmann:

*Hi LT! I've been in a rut lately and wanted to reach out to someone. God brought you to mind. Do you know of anyone who does grief counseling, or if simply talking to you might do me some good? It's hard to share sometimes, but sharing usually does me good. These little ruts aren't new to me, but this one is lasting longer than usual. Time after time I've seen God's faithfulness and I'll keep seeing such as I keep going, but sometimes we each need help in keeping one foot in front of the other. Hope it's okay reaching out to you!*

I've known Lamar Trieschmann for a few years now and have seen how anyone who meets his family automatically falls in love with all of them. Lamar and Jennifer have two girls named Claire and Maggie. This special family and the McAlister's are friends and Lamar is the pastor who did LK's celebration of life service. I graduated with Claire and Maggie, and Claire and I kicked it off our senior year, sharing homecoming memories together. As I look back, at the same time that God closed the door on my friendship with LK, He was also opening a door to a new friendship with Claire. One year, we celebrated "LK's Heavenly homecoming" together and that memory encourages me still today. Especially on those days that I don't want to celebrate. My head knows that in Christ, I always have a reason to celebrate, but it's my heart that needs to work on its memory skills.

On that particular January day, Claire and I shared ice cream and I brought mini chocolate striped cookies to our outing, because both were Lila's favorites. Giving her those, along with raviolis and french fries would make her one happy camper! I'm thankful for a beautiful memory shared with Claire on an "unbeautiful" day. On the flip of Claire, there's her sister Maggie, who I didn't get the opportunity to get to know as much but we did share a class during our senior year. I remember her using her beautiful gift of singing at LK's celebration of life, and the description of Lila that I used at the beginning of this book.

In the blur of the days after LK went running to Heaven, we were over visiting Misty and unexpectedly a "basket of thoughtfulness" was dropped off at the front door. I suppose we weren't in the main living area, because no one answered the door but somehow we found the basket on the front porch when we were leaving. God used such a simple act of kindness to touch our hearts in a noteworthy way. Jennifer is known in my book for her simple acts of kindness, she did the same action a few times on my birthday.

Even though the Trieschmanns aren't close family friends and I went months or even years without talking to any of them, God still brought LT to my jumble of thoughts when I was experiencing a low point. And I'll always be beyond thankful. I remember Lamar reaching out to me shortly after LK's celebration of life with a simple message letting me know he would be there whenever I needed someone to talk to. Fast forward 6 years later and I find blessing upon blessings every time I get an opportunity to visit with LT. He gives me a safe place to share my emotions, to share Lila Kate, and I usually learn a fun fact from the Bible. Hearts like LT's are what God uses to keep me going! With this encounter, I see again how God is so good at placing the right person in my path at the right time.

## Adventure #38 – April 20, 2021

In the midst of a struggle, I can still be thankful. I don't have to be thankful for distress, but I can still be thankful. God has given me more than enough blessings and His blessings are new each and every day! As the song goes, "God gives and takes away. Blessed be the name of the Lord." Can you imagine ancient Job singing this song that I am singing, too? Are you? Job was the famous one who had basically an earthquake and tornado all in the same day, with unprepared "see ya laters" to multiple loved ones. Not to mention that those loved ones were indeed his children, no doubt increasing the emotional turmoil Job was experiencing.

Recently, I explored Psalm 138. In the text, I see David thanking God in the midst of his struggle, which was my original purpose for writing, but that song took me for a loop to ole Job. David isn't thanking God for the struggle, but he is thankful. I noted six different things he was thankful for and I can be thankful for those same aspects. I'm sharing three below:

**1) God's steadfast love.**

Isn't there a quote somewhere that reads along the lines of "God loves us all as if we were each His favorite." Doesn't it put a pep in one's self to be someone's favorite? Sure, don't let such go to one's head but instead let such go to the heart and walk confidently singing "Jesus loves me" (and my neighbor). Because He does.

**2) God's faithfulness.**

When I experience emotional dips, an important task that is key for me is to recall how God has been faithful, because He has! Time and time again. His faithfulness does really reach to the clouds (Psalm 36). God has been faithful and God will continue to be faithful. His faithfulness doesn't erase the struggle to vanish, but His faithfulness shows me that I can continue to trust Him with the struggle.

**3) God is above all.**

The image of Paul in jail writing his letter to the church in Philippi flutters my thoughts here! Paul surely wasn't in love with his prison cell but He was still loving God and others from afar. I think Paul knew He couldn't love God on his own, because he's the one who wrote something along the lines of "nothing good dwells in me," which is the case for me, too. Actually that's the case for all of man which makes the gospel such a beautiful gift for the person who receives it. So while Paul knew he couldn't love God nor others on his own, once he realized how God loved even him (the worst of sinners) he was then able to walk in such love. He walked in love even when he was confined to his jail cell. Paul realized his personal struggles were being used by God to advance the gospel and help others walk closer to Christ, so Paul was alright with continuing to struggle. He had the gospel in addition to his struggle, so he knew God was bigger than his struggle. His perspective was healthy and not self-seeking just as he writes in his letter. He was definitely one who practiced what he preached.

## Adventure #39 – April 30, 2021

What is my reader thankful for today? The practice of thankfulness is seen throughout the Bible as a key element in a child of God's life. It can be challenging to be thankful in the midst of heartache and distress, but through David's writings in the Psalms I see him give thanks over and over in the midst of his struggle. Psalms 107 serves as an almost mirror image and clearly paints the picture that no given situation or no one is too far from God's love.

2 Chronicles 20 involves King Jehoshaphat as he gave thanks too in the midst of struggling. I studied this passage for Sunday school a while ago but it has impacted me to the degree that I thought I should share about it right here in my book! I'll encourage you to go read for yourself King Jehoshaphat's adventure because this will only serve as a sneak peek and my perspective. Plus, it's always healthy to go

explore a story for yourself when it's referenced in a book or even a sermon. Always go explore and make sure it's true!

King Jehoshaphat gets word of enemies invading the land and his response is to seek God. He doesn't only seek God but he gets others to do so, too. His faith is seen by taking the action of fasting. The king's prayer overviews some of God's character, his promises, and his faithfulness. All the while it's a prayer of distress as he is crying out to God knowing that he'll "hear and save." The people are gathered and Jahaziel speaks saying he has heard from God. This seems odd in our day but remember these people didn't have all of scripture like today so God's primary way of speaking was through people. In response the king praised, thanked, and obeyed God—even before victory was seen.

There are a handful of tidbits I took away from this story…

1) Admitting the struggle and fear is a natural reaction to a great multitude.

2) Our response to fear or other discomforts is key. Run to the Father!

3) Faith requires action.

4) One can't do hard stuff alone and we are made to seek God together!

5) Praise God even before the victory. (How much more can our hearts be full of praise, knowing what we know about Jesus' cross and resurrection)??

The Israelites probably thought "really, you want us to sing and thank God before we win over the bad guys?" The text tells me that the Israelites felt completely powerless and were clueless about what to do. Yet their eyes were on God! He would fight for them and He wanted them not to be afraid. My key verse here is verse 12: "For we are powerless against this great horde that is coming against us. We do not know what to do, but our eyes are on you." I absolutely love that verse! Because how many times do I (or my reader) feel like I'm in between a rock and a hard place! I promise you that that's what grief feels like at times! But the key is to keep my eyes upon Jesus! I fail at this daily, but it's a task of changing my perspective from focusing on my pain and attempting to fix my eyes on Him. Being ready to live my life that's not really mine, but ultimately His. And that truth affects how I view myself, my circumstances, and even others. King Jehoshaphat, knew God was/is the King of all kings. Not very many of Israel's kings knew such, but this one did and his actions showed it.

## Adventure #40 – May 13, 2021

Throughout this book I've made reference to being involved with a non-profit organization called The CALL which stands for "Children of Arkansas Living for a Lifetime." In a sentence, it's the hands and feet of Jesus coming together to love on children in foster care. Their mission statement is as follows: "to educate, equip, and encourage the Christian community to provide a future and a hope for the children in foster care." It is a statewide, faith based, 501c3, Christian Nonprofit organization founded in 2007 in Pulaski County, that is now currently active in 50 counties in Arkansas. They receive no state funding, so they wholly rely on donations from individuals, churches, and corporate donors, fundraising, and grant writing.

As I shared, right after LK ran to Heaven, the McAlister's opened their home and their hearts to experience being a foster family and of course I wiggled myself into babysitting regularly and we all quickly developed a little bond with each child. That's the first I heard about The CALL, besides learning that our church supports the organization. But then, I suppose one conversation is good about leading to the next though, when it involves the best two ingredients of time and love. Both can be used in big ways, especially in God's hands!

My "why" for involvement with The CALL involves the harsh reality of being forced to let go of Lila Kate's little hand as she ran up ahead to Heaven. Through volunteering with The CALL, God has opened my heart more and more as I attempt to let Lila Kate's legacy of love flow from my heart! When my mom and I began volunteering more, I didn't realize how God would use such a task to aid in the healing process. I was simply attempting to love more, and while I hope I do so more and more each day, God has also used this season to help me move forward with my grief. A big part of that has been due to getting involved with The CALL. I love and ache for Lila Kate more and more each day sometimes, but I also delight in pouring Jesus' love (and LK's love) on other little souls who so desperately want to be loved more!

May 30, 2020

*Why are my emotions all twisted? It's similar to what David says in Psalm 46. He turns his hope to God and off the situation at hand. God is teaching me the same, yet I will say one can still hurt and still hope. It's like what Paul says, we don't grieve like those who don't have any hope. Nonetheless, I want an LK hug! It's the nagging hurt that comes and goes, yet is always there. I know, it's confusing. LK and I have been social distancing from each other for too long! And this COVID stuff is heck. But with all this time, I've been asking God to help me expand His story more by expanding my story more. We'll see. I want God to use me to comfort others while pointing them to God who is the Father of all comfort. I want God to use me to encourage others while again pointing them to God who is the God of Encouragement! I'm thankful for God's comfort and encouragement which lately has been through Cody. His friendship to me this season honestly encourages me greatly. This year for my birthday, we tackled a summer project together which involved surprising a few kiddos in foster care with a basket of fun summer toys. I had a blast and it's definitely a noteworthy birthday memory. After we finished, we had birthday dinner on the patio and found out that we don't simply tolerate each other but we tolerate each other in the best way! God will always use Cody to remind me that God can use pain to do something good!*

## Adventure #41 – May 15, 2021

Faith in God allows me to feel those tough emotions and know that this pain isn't wasted when it's in God's hands. Faith doesn't erase the pain. Faith doesn't always give the outcome that prayer wants. Faith is a secure resting while putting one foot in front of the other even when the pain isn't erased nor the outcome isn't as expected. This past week, when I was visiting with LT he gave me a sneak peek into his sermon for the weekend and it was entitled "Nothing is Wasted." The story of Joseph skimmed my thoughts and appeared in my reading the following day, so obviously God wanted me to visit Joseph in my writing time! Joseph was on his own grief journey, too. While not necessarily the grief of a loved one, I'll say he had to be grieving the loss of his familiar lifestyle. He's the one that basically went from being the most favorable to the least favorable in a matter of moments, yet he was continually highly favored by God through it all. The same is true for my reader. He is with you, just like He was with Joseph, and He has a unique way of setting up those appointments with people. That can literally be His hand at work in your life, similar to the way He did with Joseph!

Joseph's story stands out to me because of the dramatic ups and downs he experienced, yet I clearly see by the end of the story how he would agree "Nothing is Wasted." In fact, he utters the words "As for you, you meant evil against me, but God meant it for good…" (Genesis 50:20). God had a specific reason for all the ugly and by the end of the story Joseph sees the specific reason: "to bring it about that many people should be kept alive, as they are today." (Genesis 50:20).

So as I approach the end of this book, I already see the similarities that Joseph saw, too. On that January day, death was a rude entry to the McAlister family and sometimes daily I have my "shadow of death" moments. Death was meant to destroy me but instead Jesus destroyed it upon the cross and now death doesn't have the final say. Christ has the final say with His glorious resurrection, which I share even today, and will one day share in full. The enemy meant evil, but God meant it for good in the big picture.

## Adventure #42 – May 20, 2021

Lila Kate will always be my forever friend and my absolute favorite friend to take pictures with, yet day by day, and sometimes moment by moment, I'll attempt to put one foot in front of the other! When I do I'll continue to be amazed at how God shows up continually and sometimes in the unusual. He is too good about dusting my path with specific hearts that He uses to speak words of encouragement into my life and to simply be there! I've learned to never underestimate the comfort He can bring through someone simply showing up. It doesn't have to be a physical presence, sometimes it might look like a simple text message which is right on time or a FaceTime chat. The small verbs that one does for another person can be used as big verbs in God's hands! And it's a big blessing to have hearts that enter into another person's pain, not trying to tape over the hurts, but simply watching how God is still good at healing broken hearts. It's not a process to be rushed, I remind myself. I think it's a process which God delights in. It's a process that can teach one to rely more upon Him and others, while less upon self. It's a process that involves a healthy mixture of laughter and tears. It's a process that can open new doors which God can continue to shine His light through, because His light can shine in the darkness! It's a process of learning how to shift my focus off of what I can see and fixing my eyes upon what He might be up to through all of this! It's a process I'm still working on!

When I allow my thoughts to dwell upon the ugliness of not being able to experience the "growing up" years that we would've been able to share with LK, I quickly grow ill and cold. I literally sink in disgust as I feel myself doing as I type. These little "grief bombs" are usually unexpected and drop at the most random moments. I'm confident Satan wants to take me out with such and I'm confident that God wants to do something only He can do. Meanwhile, again God sparks my memory of Peter walking on water, from a recent Sunday school lesson, and it was when Peter's attention was fixed on his temporary problem that he began to sink. In contrast, when Peter reached for the eternal, Jesus strengthened Peter and he was able to walk forward in the struggle. Peter walked in the struggle. Peter walked in the pain. God didn't remove the storm immediately. Maybe God was teaching Peter to trust Him more and more, as God is teaching me the same. God is teaching me these words, penned by Tim Charlies: "My faith, my anchor, has held, but not because I have been rowing hard, not because I have been steering well, not because I am made of rugged stuff, not because I am a man of mighty faith. It has held fast because it is held firm in the nail-scarred hands of the one who died and rose for me. He, by his grace, has held me safe thus far, and he, by his grace, will hold me to the end. I have every confidence that my anchor will hold—that my anchor will be held—until he at last delivers me to that safe harbor far across these troubled seas."

## Adventure #43 – May 23, 2021

Twenty-five years old. My 25th birthday was yesterday. What would I tell my younger self? Maybe it would go something like this: look for God's bright little surprises in the dark, because they are always there. God is continually working for His child's good. Continually. Yet time after time, I fall into worry, doubt, and fear. But still, time after time, He proves himself faithful again. Is the picture of the Israelites crossing your memory now?

Let's face it, my first thoughts leading up to my birthday were: birthdays are for best friends to be together and I don't know why I don't have a memory of LK being with me on my birthday. The single thought that birthdays are for best friends is challenging enough, but the graduation hype this time of the year makes it even more so. But God not only will love me through it, He loves me in it!

Yes, even on the happiest days, I can still feel the tug of Lila missing something with me. These thoughts are overwhelming and this graduation hype is triggering hard to swallow memories of my senior year when Lila Kate ran up to Heaven. Not to mention the fact of not being able to create any kindergarten graduation memories with that little love bug! Yes, that's how grief works at times. It tends to dog pile, especially when it's all one can focus on. Regardless of grief or not, that's a rule of thumb for life in general: focus on the pain and the pain gets bigger, but focus on the possibilities that God can do with the pain and you'll be amazed by His purpose through the pain.

So once I had my personal pity party, I was ready for my actual party. I could've cared less about having company over but I knew if we didn't my pity party would've continued and I would've regretted the fact that we didn't have friends over. I know I'm complicated to love at times, but God is still good at giving me friends who I can call family and we laughed and made beautiful memories!

God obviously knew the challenges I was experiencing this year on my birthday, so He also gave me not one but two unexpected surprises. Both of which involved Lila Kate, I'll share one here. One of the beautiful surprises was a LK picture which I had never seen before. It was Friday morning, the day before my birthday, and I was engrossed with placing letters together for a writing adventure. At the exact moment I was finished, an alert popped up and it was a distant friend sharing with me the photo of God's amazing little child! The one He graciously shared with us for a few short years, because she ultimately belongs to Him first. As do we all. The photo made me shed a few tears because I was so overwhelmed by God's goodness with the timing of this picture. It was something only God could've done and He did it perfectly!

# Adventure #44 – June 4, 2021

There's not a bone within me, all 206 of them, that would wish for LK to be back on this sinful planet but I would go to her in a heartbeat! Maybe half a heartbeat sometimes! But God is still working! He's always working. He is still igniting fires of hearts to burn for only Him. He is still comforting, strengthening, and helping through His word, His people, and simply himself. He's still the one true God, which means He's still above all else. As I'm wrapping this book up, I wanted to share one of my favorite Old Testament adventures, Habakkuk—one of the twelve minor prophets. They're all pretty interesting to study in my opinion! Each book is small, hence the name "minor," but each one plays a major role in God's unfolding plan of Christ coming into the world to save mankind.

Zach Windahl, who is the author of *The Bible Study*, wrote the following:

*Habakkuk was a man who questioned everything. He wrestled with God until he received an answer that was fitting for his narrow perspective. But Habakkuk wasn't God, so some things would never make sense. Same with today. We can wrestle with as much as we want, but in the end, some things will remain a mystery.*

Habakkuk wasn't alone in his questioning. Others in the Bible like David, Job, and even Jesus had their box of questions, too. Matter of fact, I have mine as well. But similar to Job, maybe God has questions for me, too. By the end of Job's story, I see God ask Job big questions such as "Where were you when I laid the foundation of the earth? Tell me, if you have an understanding. Have you commanded the morning since your days began, and caused the dawn to know its place? Have you comprehended the expanse of the earth? Declare, if you know all this." (Job 38:4,12,18).

Not too long ago in one of my visits, LT brought Job to the table and our conversation triggered the line JD Grear had written: "God often provides no explanation for his ways, but instead he gives a revelation of his character." That's exactly what one sees with God's response to Job. It's not what Job expected, but it was what he needed. Similar to God's response to Habbakkuk, it probably wasn't what Habakkuk had in mind. God was raising up the Chaldeans who were an enemy of Israel, which stirred more questions in Habakkuk's limited mindset. God didn't want Habakkuk to fear, but instead in chapter two God literally commanded anxious Habakkuk to watch, write, and wait. I love these three "w's" for obvious reasons, but they're actually tricky and it shows us that waiting is never doing nothing. God rarely calls His child to do nothing.

I'm not making note of every detail in Habakkuk, but I'll close by sharing again my favorite lines our pastor shared with me as the words summarize the book most clearly. I think someone shared it with him, so now it's my turn to share with you and then guess what? It's your turn to go read Habakkuk and share this encouraging word with another: "One may not see what God is doing, one may not understand what God is doing, but one can always trust what God is doing."

By the end of Habakkuk's back and forth conversation with God, Habakkuk comes to the conclusion that he's simply not God! Habakkuk uses the images at the end of chapter three (which were all very needed in this lifestyle) to describe the joy and strength God gave him regardless of the situation that was cycling at the current time.

## Adventure #45 – June 6, 2021

As stated specifically in Adventure #4, "that girl taught me more about love in three days than I had ever known." That's the legacy Lila Kate left upon this big beautiful world that is tainted with the nastiness of sin. The young boy who made this comment was a church camp volunteer whom the McAlisters hosted one summer. During his short stay, he experienced that which we all crave, love. He experienced the "Lila Kate love." The love which her daddy described with these words: "Lila's love didn't say no, Lila's love didn't say maybe. Lila's love was simply love."

Yes, of course she had her moments, like the instances when she told Thomas, "I mad." Or the instances of her repeatedly pulling off her oxygen right after her mom or dad finished reapplying the stickers. She was a typical child who threw fits when told "no," which was a word highly used in her vocabulary. She went through the phases of pulling glasses off of other beautiful faces. I remember her daddy literally getting himself "Lila-proof glasses" which did the trick for at least himself! We used the phrase "hands down" when Lila reached for our glasses and we would say the words as we firmly lowered her hands away from our face.

But when people think of Lila, most automatically recall that small yet powerful four letter word of which Our Savior is the ultimate example. None will ever fill His shoes, nor needs to because what He accomplished through his cross and his resurrection will always be enough. As His child I can rest assured in that unfailing, unwavering, and unending love but in the same sentence I realize He commands repeatedly that we love others. In fact, love is to be a mark of His children. The way we love others is what will show others that we belong to Him (John 13:35). Jesus doesn't love us simply for us to love ourselves more and more, but Jesus loves us for us to love others more and more.

So that's what I attempt to focus on doing these days: loving and loving more. Yes, hopefully more writing too and maybe I love that more, but loving people is the essence of what I'm referring to. Just love. Love. Love can be hard, Jesus loved hard. But where would I be without His love? And because of that love poured out in red, surely I can love a little bit more here and there. As I approached the end of my first edit through this book, God gave me an opportunity to love some more in a very special way. A baby girl who *was* in foster care. This adventure continues with my eight-week reflection of my time with her!

It's eight weeks to the day. Eight weeks ago, I met this almost three-month-old baby girl and completely fell in love. Of course I thought of Lila when I met her and many times there after! So many times since meeting this baby, I have added to my "why" box for God which I know is pointless but I know He cares, too. I questioned why God took a child from a healthy family and not one from an unhealthy family. Yes, I know all children belong to God first but still I played with this question. I questioned why I didn't meet Lila when she was itty bitty. I questioned why I don't remember when Lila first rolled over or any of those milestones for that matter. But thank goodness we do have her first steps on video. I can also reflect on so many more times I saw God's goodness and faithfulness with my own eyes. I'm constantly taking pictures because it's what Lila and I did and plus it's capturing this little one, too. I'm praying that I'll be able to share these pictures with her one day and share a lot more memories with her, too. But I don't stop praying for her momma because she needs prayer, too. It's a constant tug-of-war with "our plan" and "God's plan," but I attempt to rest in the truth that God's plan is complete. So yes, this is another small tool which God has used and it's exhausting and exciting all at the same time—as most of life is. It's falling into sinful traps because it's so easy to become envious. We learn to protect our hearts and guard against sin while thanking God for His underserved amazing grace.

When someone other than me held or played with the baby creating giggles or baby talk, this created a rush of negative energy for me. I know it's pretty silly, but these simple actions triggered what Lila and I used to do and instead of happy memories, I felt locked with anger that probably looked like envy. And yes I have my happy memories but I also have this war against my flesh. Quickly I learned to remove myself from the area if someone else has the baby so I can do better with that. I have trouble expressing my feelings by talking sometimes, so these types of situations can result in a river from my eyes which can turn into an emotional disaster if I'm not careful. But I'm still learning. I'm still healing. I'm still moving forward. One step at a time.

## Grief/LK Tidbits

As I shared before, the anticipation of LK's birthday tends to get the best of me every year. So I've been trying to do something positive in memory of her and in 2020 she would've turned 11 years old so I compiled 11 little "LK tidbits" or lessons that I've learned over the past years with her living in heaven.

Some of these tidbits intersect with one another and there are a handful more which include: we need each other, life is the fast lane even if one doesn't realize it, and never underestimate the power of a random check in text/call from a friend or even simply someone's presence. However, these eleven tidbits are the ones I felt like God wanted me to share! By no means have I mastered these lessons, and by all means I would've loved to learn these lessons outside of LK's homecoming, but as I read time and time again, "not my will, but yours, be done."

1) There's no such thing as too many laughs in one day, even the smallest moments, because really the small moments are the big! Our favorite thing to laugh at was when I built block towers and LK waited ever so patiently to tumble the tower down! When the tower crashed, we both chuckled. Now I'm the one waiting patiently for when we can play together again. Patience is harder than hard stuff.

2) There's no such thing as too many pictures in one day. Yes, there can be, but regardless pictures are priceless because they serve to me as a "virtual playdate" sometimes. I remember being asked why I took a handful of pictures when hanging out with Lila and not knowing, but now I know exactly why. In a way, I think pictures are how God somewhat prepared me for seeing Lila go to Heaven—which

was ugly but at the same time beautiful.

3) There's no such thing as too many hugs in one day. LK was known for big hugs! On most Fridays, she would run to the door after school to greet me with a tight squeeze! I would almost give anything to get another LK hug! I realize now a hug from the right person can dismiss the ache even if it's just for a second—it's a second less hurting.

4) There's such a thing as experiencing beauty with the ugly. Death is ugly and grief is ugly. Grief is death's ugly friend. Yet Jesus is acquainted with both. That's the essence of why Christ came, He came to destroy the power of death. He came because it was ugly. He'll come back because it's ugly. But in the meantime, He still does beautiful and one way He does this is through our weak, fragile, and sinful hearts, which he came to redeem and is redeeming day by day. It is a beautiful fight. Yes, fights can be beautiful.

5) There's such a thing as moving forward while still cherishing memories and creating more memories. This is an extra tough one but so needed along the journey. It's tempting to compare journeys but it's not what is needed. The Bible compares life to a race as well as a walk, which is confusing to me. But regardless, life is moving forward and doesn't really care if one wants it to or not. Life is still moving forward and that means God is still working. So one must continue to work, too; because we each are His workmanship.

6) There's such a thing as blessings in disguise. This ties back to Adventures #4 and #5, in a way because it too is beautiful and requires one to move forward even if it's baby steps. It's sometimes jaw dropping to see how good God is at weaving together different people's paths and how one person's pain can be used to help someone else. Even more than that, God's full goodness simply isn't fully seen by one's eye but

still He is beyond good at giving us glimpses of his goodness and calling us to gaze at the unseen—all while keeping two feet upon this earth.

7) There's such a thing as still enjoying life, even in the midst of pain. I feel like I'm pep talking myself on some of these little one liners, but that's the way it is at times! In the beginning of this journey with grief, I felt selfish for experiencing sparks of happiness. Like why laugh because doesn't that mean "I'm happy?" Well, yes and no. I'll never be "happy" about such a tragedy, but I'll say overall I have a happy/joyful/bubbling personality. Sure I have my off days or weeks, for which I've learned that laughter is really a healthy medicine and there's no doubt that LK laughs in Heaven! I will too, one day. But for now I can still laugh here and besides what was my #1 tidbit? There's no such thing as too many laughs in one day! While there's definitely a time to cry, there's a time to laugh too! And sometimes a healthy mixture of both!

8) God gave us lots of emotions and sometimes one can feel those multiple emotions at once and it's overwhelming in every way. Emotions in themselves are not wrong, they are a part of being human, but it's the reaction to them that can be tricky. My personality is bubbling and cheerful, so when the devil wants to use the heaviness of grief to weigh me down I have a tendency to be hard on myself. I want to feel what I show others. Most of the time others see my happiness and joy, because it's there too. It's there because my home is Heaven and in the meantime God will continue to shower His amazing surprises on me, in small and big ways. The devil can use my grief in a negative way, which pulls me away from God and others, but God can use my grief, too. I'm still in His hands so that means this grief can rest there, too. The concept of resting and walking in faith can be confusing at times because we are called to "rest," but not simply called to do nothing. There's balance in everything.

9) When "IDKs" are flooding one's mind, just go with what one does know. God spells out countless truths in His word. Just last week I was talking with Cade about the aging process in Heaven or even if there is such a thing there. We both weren't sure, but the blessing of this particular friendship is that we were able to close the conversation with the truth of Heaven being beyond beautiful anyhow. In the meantime, God still has assignments with each of our names on them, we are sure of that. The special blessings of meaningful friendships are sometimes found in difficulty, and we aren't created to fix each other or have all the answers, but to keep loving each other through the highs and the lows.

10) Patience. Big one. Lots of people say I'm patient and it's usually when I'm with the kiddos, but honestly I have to fight for patience. It's a fruit of the Spirit, so when I'm in step with God's leading, only then am I patient! Regardless, I've learned various aspects of patience through this journey: patience with self, patience with others, and patience with God. Yep, all three. All three are equally hard and equally important. When I experience my little lows, I work on patience. When I don't understand why another person is responding in a certain way or why God isn't moving in another person's life the way that I think he should, I work on patience. When I'm simply ready for Heaven, I work on patience. I have seen His perfect timing again and again, so I know I'll continue to see it again and again.

11) Life continues until God says it's finished. Life continues—that's the hardest part of grief. But I'm so thankful that the words Jesus uttered on the cross were "It is finished," instead of "He's finished." Yes, with the cross and the resurrection, Jesus completed the work needed to secure my salvation but by no means is He completely finished working.

## Closing Thoughts

Lila Kate is literally missed by me all the time and I know some others can say the same; especially her mommy and daddy. Even in my happiest moments, I still catch myself wondering why she can't share the happiness with me as best friends tend to do. Laugh, take pictures, and whatever else best friends enjoy doing together. Sure I realize that she's happy in Heaven and her joy is complete, but that doesn't make my grief vanish. Yes that truth definitely changes how I grieve on a day to day basis, but this grief won't vanish until Heaven and I try to be okay with that. It's as Paul says, I grieve with hope. Hope in Christ. He is the only reason for hope. Hope. That's the four letter word that is like a breath of fresh air. Hope. One day I won't need hope nor faith, but today I do. Hope, faith, and also love. Love. Love is the greatest and again this takes me back to "LK's celebration of life" service as I shared previously. That was where I thought everything wasn't going to be okay, where I thought I could never enjoy this gift called life anymore, and where I definitely thought I couldn't love another little girl as much as I loved and still love Lila. Thankfully God hasn't left me to my own nature and His love for me empowers me to continue forward, and when I do, I find more blessings in disguise.

As I write my closing thoughts to this book, my tag line has been pain with purpose is still pain but it's still purpose, too. And again, the date is approaching all too fast on the calendar. Seven years! Seven years of LK running around in Heaven, and personally, that has been way too long. Seven years since we had our weekly playdate where we escaped in countless story books, built soft block towers, and played with the kitchen set with dolls. Seven years since we made each other laugh or took a picture together. Seven years is too long. I could probably keep my list going even with memories I didn't get to create with Lila Kate that I ache for, too. Like the simple memories of going to the zoo, seeing Santa, riding a big girl bike, saying more complete words, and thousands more! All these aspects are included in my hurt and can be emotionally paralyzing at times, if not physically, too. And yes this is seven years later and yes seven years is still too long. But back to my tag line: pain with purpose is still pain, but it's still purpose, too.

Twenty-One Adventures & More

# NOTES

**Adventure 13**
Michael R. Emlet, *Saints, Sufferers & Sinners*, p. 88
Jamie Lusko, *Bloom* (Suicide Awareness)

**Adventure 14**
Lindsey Wheeler, *Sacred Tears*, p. 61

**Adventure 19**
https://www.challies.com/articles/my-anchor-holds/

**Adventure 21**
https://www.ndss.org/about-down-syndrome/down-syndrome/

**Adventure 24**
Levi Lusko, *Through the Eyes of a Lion* p. 152

**Adventure 26**
J.D. Greear, *Not God Enough*

**Adventure 27**
J.D. Greear, *Not God Enough*

**Adventure 28**
https://herviewfromhome.com/church-is-hard/

**Adventure 28**
Dennis L. Apple, *Life After the Death of my Son*

**Adventure 42**
https://www.challies.com/articles/my-anchor-holds/

**Bio**
https://www.cdc.gov/ncbddd/cp/facts.html

# LK MEMORIES

**Lora Whelan** - My first meeting with LK was at your house when we came for a visit! As soon as she entered the house her face lit up and she ran to her favorite person - you! Anyone could tell the special bond you two had. There was laughter and running and a sense you had just met a special little person.

**Jan Wright ("Mimi")** - The last Christmas we were all at the cabin. It couldn't have been more perfect. She loved riding the ranger with her brother, sister, & all her cousins. The smile I can see her now. Laughing out loud was so sweet. She was scared of Biggies mounted Turkey on the wall. I lifted her up for a closer look & she grabbed me around the neck and said, "dat scares me Mimi"… love those hugs!

**Susan Breitenberg** - I remember seeing her for the first time at the middle school…Skip brought her up to see Misty and the rest of the middle school crew. She was just a precious tiny tot and little did I know, she would make her way into your heart, and anyone that met her. Happiest little girl that radiated love all around her. Also the way she loved your senior homecoming flowers! Y'all created so much joy around you by smelling each flower over and over again!

**Jennifer Trieschman** - I do have a special memory about Lila Kate. I was a nanny for a family here in town for eight years. Their oldest son was right around the same age as LK. A couple of times we saw her at the park with her granddad. She didn't really know me, but both times she ran over to us and said "hi!" She was the friendliest, most effervescent little girl- it always made my day to see her!

**Joyce Breitenberg** -I don't recall meeting LK in person, but I feel that I know her through your memories and stories of her. Even though her life here on earth was short, her impact on others was powerful and long reaching, and will live on through the pages of your book.

**Dawn Gigger** - My favorite memory is singing at church with her on my lap and she just kept smiling and looking back at me.

**Rebekah Holiman** - I think some of my favorite things about her were the way she said my name. I have a stuffed monkey from her that she had named Bekah, and that was so special to me. I remember being at my grandmother's house lying in bed with my mom and she peaked her head through the door and then came over to us and climbed up in bed with us and just made us laugh by making funny faces.

**David Puckett** - I went by their house one evening to pick Audrey up from a sleep over. All the girls were in the back somewhere and Skip and I were talking at the kitchen table. All of a sudden we heard footsteps approaching. It was LK. She was wearing nothing but bubbles from her bath. She jumped in my arms, gave me a big hug, & said, "Hi Bob!" To this day we don't know why but that's why I dressed up as Bob the Builder that year at the 5K.

**Betty Hightower** - I love the memory of watching her siblings, cousins, and friends embrace her. She was so loved by all ages and she loved BIG in return. I can still feel those pats on the back.

**Anthony Brunet** - Our favorite LK race memory was in 2017 on St. Patricks Day and we had our whole family together. We got to run and cheer everyone on together as a family, that's what makes LK race the best!

# ACKNOWLEDGEMENTS

**God** - I thank God for sharing Lila Kate with us for four and a half years. The time wasn't long enough but I thank God for the time we had together. I thank God for the ability of writing of which He gave me and for the countless people who He has allowed to cross my path at just the right time.

**The McAlister Family** - I don't know quite where to begin with this "thank you!" It seems as though "thank you" can never be enough! I thank you guys for sharing beautiful Lila Kate with me and we thank God for sharing her with all of us! Keep doing one of the hardest things any parent is forced to do. Love you guys more!

**My mom, dad, Ethan and Melissa** - Thank you all for loving me through everything; especially through the process of completing this book. For me to be present in our moments together and for me to be working through my timeline of this book presented its obstacles some days. But we all did survive! Love you guys big!

**Ashley Wiggins** - Thank you for devoting so much time into this project. The ample time you spent doing my first edit and giving me feedback was exactly what I needed at the time. I'm thankful that God reconnected us through this process and to share Lila Kate with you virtually was a gift to me!

**Jeff Hill** - Thank you for being here since basically the beginning of my journey through grief. You've seen me when I thought I couldn't go forward anymore and you've also seen what God can do when we choose to go forward, too. To this day, I can thank you for always having listening ears and simply walking along with me through the ups and the downs. I thank you for continually redirecting my heart to

God's words and the timely encouragement that you share with me. Love you.

**Lamar Trieschmann** - Thank you for coming alongside me as I finished my rough draft and sticking around even in this particular season. Jennifer and you are both blessings in disguise to me and will always be. There's no doubt that God used LK to bring us together. I love you both so much! LT, the time you regularly share with me is a vital encouragement to me and something I look forward to! God continually uses you to do my heart good.

**Tim Pool** - Thank you so much for being a good family friend to us! You were one of the first people that I shared the book idea with and you helped me fill in some vital holes especially in my bio. The encouragement you shared with me as I went down that path particularly was very needed as I continued forward.

**Janis Bremer -** Thank you for reading through my book and voicing your suggestions and making minor adjustments along the way.

**Janna Barber** - Again I see God placing the right person at the right time in my path! That day when dad was at lunch with your brother, I wasn't thinking God might've been making another connection in the "writing world" for me! But He did. You were very patient with me and I value your feedback.

**Brittany Carter** - Thank you for doing a final read through and a "quick sweep" through my book! I'm glad that Brandi Bettis shared with me your contact and that you were willing to voice your feedback as well as making adjustments along the way.

# ABOUT THE AUTHOR

On May 22, 1996, I apparently wasn't quite ready to see God's great big world. There were early signs that something was not exactly right. I would experience multiple episodes of bradycardia, which is a slower than normal heart rate. My birth story shaped my life and influenced my relationships and perspective.

The early signs should have resulted in an expedient delivery process so I could be placed on oxygen. Due to the doctor's failure to recognize, or his disregard of the distress of my heart rate, I experienced prolonged bradycardia. This lasted approximately six minutes. Consequently, a vacuum extraction (an extreme form of helping a baby through the birth canal) was completed. However, the doctor exceeded the number of recommended pulls during the vacuum extraction, resulting in a hematoma on the left side of my head (a formation of blood under the skin which usually results when a vein or artery becomes injured), and a broken right clavicle. Due to the intense stress during birth, I quickly developed seizure activity. I spent five days in the ICU where, thankfully, the best nurses took care of me. After having many unpleasant thoughts about the doctor who delivered me, I can then see that shortly thereafter God placed the right people in my path at the right time.

After coming home from the hospital, while giving me a bath one evening, my mom noticed unusual tightness in my right arm which triggered some "mommy questions." I also didn't seem very stable while sitting, so this triggered more "mommy questions." My pediatrician recommended having me evaluated by a local Early Childhood Intervention Specialist at the age of nine months old. I qualified for PT (Physical Therapy), OT (Occupational Therapy), and Speech Therapy, which I probably started by the time I was one-year old. Due to my dad's job, we moved from Texas to Arkansas when I was eighteen months old. Here I had better opportunities with regard to therapy options. By age two or three, I was given the diagnosis of Spastic diplegia Cerebral Palsy, which it's commonly referred to as simply "CP." This is the description of my diagnosis:

*Allie is a delightful, cooperative three-year-old whose communication and motor development is severely limited. She appears to have age-appropriate receptive language and conceptual abilities, which is fortunate; however, these abilities are locked inside an expressive barrier which prevents her from functioning at an age appropriate level in her environment.*

I've learned that there are multiple types of cerebral palsy, but my type can be defined as, "muscle stiffness mainly in the legs, with the arms less affected or not affected at all. People with spastic diplegia might have difficulty walking because tight hip and leg muscles cause their legs to pull together, turn inward, and cross at the knees." This explains the unusual tightness my mom pointed out early on and probably answered a handful of questions regarding my development. This opened the door to another handful of questions about raising a daughter with CP.

In my opinion, my parents went above and beyond with raising me to be the person I am today. I know without a doubt that God chose each of us specifically for each other. I'm not the only child God handpicked for my parents, I do have a younger brother! On most days, I can't picture life without him! Thankfully, he had a much smoother delivery process and continues to pretty much go with the flow of life. He's modest, easy going for the most part, has a healthy sense of humor with a level head, and can be an extremely hard worker! I'm thankful for the hundreds of childhood memories we have with each other, and in general the good memories that I have created with family and friends throughout the years!

With my CP diagnosis, I continued PT, OT, and Speech Therapy until roughly eighth grade. I can look back and smile on my "happy" therapy memories like carrying a full cup of water across the room without spilling, repeating words back to my therapist, conquering the stairs, practicing fine motor skills with shaving cream on the mirror, and of course the big blue exercise ball.

However, therapy wasn't always peachy. I'm sure there were moments in therapy where I was literally kicking and screaming because that's the kind of day I was having; especially when I wore these fancy gloves called "hand helper" or braces on my feet that were supposedly fancy, too. I didn't tend to think either were in style. I'll admit to this day

I can have a hard head and can be very stubborn. But these therapists loved me through it, and I know each therapist played a vital role during specific seasons of my life. I had an electronic friend called a "Delta Talker" that helped me communicate, and yes this thing was indeed fancy. It was an electronic keyboard filled with pictures, and when I pressed a certain button, it would say the word. It did wonders for me!

I also recall lots of doctor visits, especially when I was younger. I have a slight case of epilepsy, a disorder in which nerve cell activity in the brain is disturbed, causing seizures, which was kept under control by daily medicine. Eventually I was (and am) seizure free! But I still remember those hateful EEG's to monitor my brain activity. Those probes are the worst, and it's a surprise that I don't remember kicking a doctor.

And too, the dreadful Botox injections that supposedly helped with my tight muscles. I don't remember if these helped me much and there were many side effects, so luckily this wasn't something I did for too long. The only bright spot in this treatment was that a free stuffed animal was included with each appointment! I also went out of the state for some doctor's appointments, specifically the hyperbaric treatments, which basically increase oxygen to the body. The highlight of these trips was a camping trip at a new campground!

As I approached middle/high school, it was tough to do therapy on a daily basis. I was and am highly functioning, so fear of falling behind during classroom instruction did cut back my therapy. I did some therapy outside of school to supplement what I wasn't getting during the school day. Besides therapy, mom always had me involved in some physical activity. I participated in something like gymnastics, swimming, working out at a local gym, or horseback riding. In general, these are all things that are healthy for anyone to do. But in my circumstances these activities were and are vital to me. Even to this day, I've learned to be adamant about working out with my trainer at a local gym doing weight training, balancing activities, and coordination exercises. I'm thankful for the accountability that having a workout trainer can offer because I need a person who can push me to continue to reach my full potential. In my opinion, we all need someone like that in different aspects of life!

In 2013, I had been out of PT for a while. My mom thought that I would continue to benefit from this therapy, so she looked around for a local PT who could work mainly on stretching. Muscle tightness continues to be one of my biggest challenges with CP as it causes discomfort at times. This is especially noticeable when I've been on my feet too long. My muscles tend to get tired sooner than is typical for most people, and my energy level tends to be depleted quickly some days. At this PT clinic, the therapist, Eddie Steadman, and I hit it off perfectly with each other. I totally loved working out with him, and we have quite the collection of memories. For example, there were times when I was supposed to be working on my jumping. But instead of jumping, I would literally face plant on the padded table—like those you see in doctor's offices, except bigger and not as tall. Most of the time we laughed once we knew that I was alright, then I would try again.

Eddie would also allow me to do some exercises along with some school-aged patients that were in rehab for a sports injury, and I suppose one thing led to another, as I started volunteering sometime in the summer during the afternoon, before I did my therapy session with Eddie. He quickly noticed my work ethic and proceeded to hire me for a job once I graduated high school. What? Fast forward 10 years and, yes, I'm still showing up at the clinic.
Sometimes I'm ready for a change of scenery, while other times I tend to think I'm right where God wants me to be. Regardless, I'll always be beyond thankful for the one-on-one

time that Eddie has poured into me throughout the years and that he took a chance by hiring me to work at his clinic! Eddie is definitely the definition of the absolute best physical therapist, who goes above and beyond for almost anyone.

I tend to think if it wasn't for my CP, God may have not had Eddie in my path. Every time I recount this small encounter of meeting him, I'm reminded that God tends to be up to more than we know or expect and He has an unusual way of crossing His child's path with the right person at the right time. And that's the sum of what I pray my reader has gathered throughout this book!